f
BUSINESS

fishy
BUSINESS

James P. Ignizio
and
Bill Ignizio

BERKLEY BOOKS, NEW YORK

This book is an original publication of The Berkley Publishing Group.

FISHY BUSINESS

A Berkley Book / published by arrangement with
the authors

PRINTING HISTORY
Berkley trade paperback edition / December 1997

The Putnam Berkley World Wide Web site address is http://www.berkley.com

ISBN   0-425-16018-1

BERKLEY®
Berkley Books are published by The Berkley Publishing Group,
a member of Penguin Putnam Inc.,
200 Madison Avenue, New York, New York 10016.
BERKLEY and the "B" design
are trademarks belonging to Berkley Publishing Corporation.

PRINTED IN THE UNITED STATES OF AMERICA
10 9 8 7 6 5 4 3 2 1

Contents

Contents

Contents

Contents

Contents

Foreword

Admit it. After checking out the title of the book you hold in your hands and flipping to the foreword, one or more of these questions is running through your mind right now:

1. Do these guys really expect me to buy into the concept of better business through *fishing*?
2. Are they serious?
3. Isn't this really just another gimmicky business book?

The answers, in order, are yes, yes, and no. Well, of course they're going to say that, you're probably thinking. But the idea of becoming a better manager through angling analogies is just too, too weird.

If you feel that way, guess what—we have something in common. When my brother Jim first approached me with the suggestion that we collaborate on *Fishy Business,* I was *not* enthusiastic. Instead of turning the idea down flat, however, I decided at least to consider the premise. I hope you'll do the same.

Foreword

Jim's explanation of how business, American style, is closely associated with war and games soon had me nodding in agreement. I knew from experience that many managers routinely pepper their casual conversations and meetings with such phrases as "we gotta hit one out of the park," "take no prisoners," and "be a team player."

One of my bosses, as a matter of fact, started off each day with a coachlike pep talk before sending us off to "score big." Sometimes he even patted me on the butt as I entered the "game"!

Other managers I've known stressed teamwork or the necessity of "waging war." Okay, score one for big brother. (Oops, there's another game analogy.) Anyhow, I bought into the idea that an awful lot of managers view business in a ballgame or battlefield context.

Still, I was *not* convinced that the idea of better business *through fishing analogies* was sound. After reading a few pages of the original outline, however, I began to realize that he just might be onto something.

Let me explain. Jim is an internationally renowned business consultant and a pioneer in the field of decision making through analogies. He knows that we learn—as well as form the basis for our decisions—by comparing a new experience with an old one. That, in a nutshell, is what an analogy is.

Unfortunately, many folks who don't even realize they routinely use analogies to arrive at their decisions, use the *wrong* kinds of business analogies (such as those associated with war and games). This can lead to big problems.

So, even though it may seem odd, the concept of fishing analogies is clearly *not* a gimmick. Rather than striving to be cute or clever, *Fishy Business* is based on sound, scientific principles. (I know, I know—it still seems WEIRD.)

One more huge hurdle remained in my personal struggle to accept the idea. Why *fishing* analogies? Why not gardening, Ping-Pong, or bird-watching?

This was not arrived at by whim. Jim considered many different activities that could be used as analogies for making sound business decisions. In the end, he was convinced that fishing was far better than other activities and infinitely supe-

Foreword

rior to the present war-and-games approach. After reading just a few pages, you'll see why.

At this point, you may well have another legitimate question: can I expect to get anything out of this book even if I don't know much about fishing?

Absolutely. That's where my contribution comes in. Having written for many national and regional outdoor publications on various angling topics for many years, I know that fishing can be puzzling. That's why the stories are kept simple. While you may encounter some terms that are unfamiliar, they are not crucial to your understanding of the story. If, out of curiosity, however, you want to know the meaning of "crankbait" or "spinning reel," a glossary of angling terms is provided.

We trust you'll find *Fishy Business* a pleasant and helpful experience. A number of nonangling readers were surprised and delighted to discover that both the fishing and business portions of the book proved enjoyable. The format is unique, but easily understood. In most chapters, we begin with a continuing fishing tale followed by a complementary business response. In several instances, the business responses refer to Jim's personal experience. So, whenever "I" appears in the business sections, it refers to Jim.

You'll also notice one or two angling adages in each fishing yarn that are matched up with appropriate business advice in the second half of the chapter. This correspondence is presented as in the example shown below. Note that a fish symbol precedes the fishing adage and a briefcase follows the business analogy.

 Don't fish for pike like you would for bass.

■ ■ ■

Know your customer.

Foreword

After three or four chapters, you'll be in the flow as you share a boat with our fishing hero, Frank, and listen in as his new friend, the somewhat mysterious O.A., generously offers angling advice that often seems surprisingly pertinent to business as well.

But enough talk. Feel the cool breeze coming off the water's surface? Hear the rustling in the branches of the towering pines that line the bank? Say, was that the splash of a big fish jumping a few yards off shore?

What are we waiting for? Let's go fishing!

—BILL IGNIZIO
Cuyahoga Falls, Ohio

Prologue

The vivid blue sky reflected on the still water of the cattail-ringed bay as a solitary angler, seated in a small rowboat, cast out a topwater lure. The deep-toned croaking of a bullfrog backed by a chorus of songbirds added a pleasant sound track to the peaceful scene.

Electronic beeping suddenly and unexpectedly disrupted the solitude. Scowling, the angler pulled a cellular phone out of the duffel bag at his feet and extended the antenna. Ned, up-and-coming junior executive, had an urgent message that just couldn't wait.

Prologue

"We can bomb Essner," he said gleefully, referring to a competing firm. "We'll outflank them with an ad campaign Don and I just worked up; it's time for the slam dunk, boss!"

The angler smiled in spite of himself at the supercharged words of his enthusiastic assistant. "Sounds fine, Ned," he said. "Let's talk some more about it tomorrow."

"We're gonna score big on this one," Ned promised before hanging up. The angler sighed, picked up his rod, and returned to fishing.

The fishing boss we've just encountered appears to lack the killer instinct of the younger man. Or maybe this single snippet in time isn't enough to reveal the true picture. Whatever the case, Ned talks of business strategies and deals as though he were describing a war or perhaps a ball game. This is not unusual.

In practice, a typical business conference often sounds like the participants are engaged in some form of "combat." The list below was compiled during a two-hour business meeting conducted at a major petrochemical firm.

PHRASE	OCCURRENCES
Don't drop the ball	4
We gotta work as a team	3
We need a quick score	2
It's the bottom of the ninth	2
Drop back ten and punt	2
Lay the wood (lumber) to it	2
Slam-dunk it	2
It's our turn at bat	1
Winners talk about winning; losers talk about the score	1
Take no prisoners	1
Nuke 'em	1
Flank 'em	1

These results are hardly unique. Try charting such comments at *your* next business meeting, and see if you don't agree.

It is obvious that little boys with war and ball games on their minds may grow up to become big businessmen . . . with war and ball games *still* on their minds. This, incidentally, may help explain why women are sometimes excluded from business "games"—or perhaps have risen *above* them. After all, many (although, certainly not all) women grew up playing with dolls, playing house, and cooperating rather than competing with one another.

But what of competition? Aren't we always competing in life and business? And must we not have a competitive spirit to survive?

Competition is, indeed, a crucial factor in most types of business endeavors. But it is far more expansive in scope than are games and war. Like fishing, competition goes on—forever. If you insist on fighting business battles on a daily basis, your time, energy, resources, and perhaps your health are wasted. This is especially true if you fight the *wrong* battles.

 Long-term goals breed long-term success—in fishing or business.

CHAPTER 1

If You Can't Drop the Putt, Drop the Game

It hadn't been a particularly good day for Frank. It had, in fact, been pretty putrid. A glance at his watch told him he had been on the lake for almost four hours without catching a single fish.

But Frank was not the kind of guy who caved in easily. It's not simply that he disliked the idea of failure; he HATED it. Despite this, his third unsuccessful outing in as many weekends, he was not ready to call it quits.

Besides, everyone from his coworkers to his wife told him he needed to learn to relax. After checking his blood pressure one day after work, his doctor agreed. Well-meaning friends and relatives offered such surefire stress-abating activities as handball, bowling, jogging, and meditation.

Frank argued that he already played golf; wasn't that enough "downtime"? Finally, a coworker and fellow golfer convinced him that golf wasn't the answer . . . for Frank, at least.

"Frank, ol' buddy," he said, after sinking a six-footer, "golf is a great sport. But I doubt if it really has a soothing effect on *you*."

Frank wasn't sure he understood. He lined up a short putt of his own and stepped back to get one final view of the green's undulations. Certain he had the right line, he stroked the ball crisply. It ended up teetering on the left side of the cup.

"Damn!" Frank berated the noncompliant golf ball. "Fall in, you lousy, little . . ."

"Does this game really make you feel better?" his partner asked. During the remainder of the round, nothing more was said on the subject.

Frank finally realized that his golfing buddy was right. He viewed golf—no matter if he played it alone or in a foursome—as competition, not relaxation. It was either Frank against the course (and he never won that one) or Frank against the other golfers in his group.

Any missed or "stupid" shot stayed with him the rest of the round, sometimes the rest of the week. He brooded over his long irons, deplored his sand-trap play, and—as we have seen—cursed his putting. Something was wrong.

That's when Frank decided to give fishing a try. Thinking back to his childhood and those restful outings at his uncle's farm pond, Frank surprised himself by discovering some pleasant memories tucked away in a forgotten corner of his mind.

This particular day would *not* be added to his list of memorable fishing jaunts. He had tried everything in the tackle box, and all with the same disappointing results. Not one fish showed even the slightest interest in anything Frank tossed out.

His wrist was tired from casting and his shoulders ached from rowing the clumsy rental boat around the lake. This was not turning out to be nearly as much fun as promised.

Mulling over these thoughts, Frank began gathering his colorful, and totally ineffective, lures and cramming them back into the tackle box. Spinnerbaits, jigs, spoons, and even a "magic" lure that some TV huckster promised would catch boat-loads of fish were in his pitiful collection.

2

Fishy Business

It takes more than a full tackle box to catch fish.

In typical Frank fashion, he had plunged headlong into fishing, reading everything he could get on the subject and even watching a gaggle of TV fishing shows each weekend. As far as he could tell, these always-successful fishermen fell into two broad groups: fishing experts with beards and fishing experts with Southern accents. (Maybe it would help if he stopped shaving and started watching reruns of *Andy Griffith*.)

A noise startled Frank, and he looked up. Several yards off his starboard bow, an angler was doing his best to subdue a thrashing fish. Frank wasn't sure, but he thought it might be a largemouth bass, and a big one, too.

After a short but spirited fight, the fisherman deftly hoisted the wriggling fish from the water. With a few practiced moves, he quickly removed the lure and gently returned the big fish to the lake.

Some guys have all the luck, Frank thought with a mixture of resentment and self-pity. He rowed off to find a new (hopefully, better) spot, not realizing that his path and that of the "lucky" bass fisherman's would soon cross again.

Golf's a game, fishing's an experience

Golf is a great game, no doubt about it. Yet, like all games, it is a highly artificial and tightly structured pursuit with a rigid set of rules and a limited selection of equipment. And, bottom line, its single-minded purpose is to get that dimpled little white ball into the cup in the fewest number of strokes.

As a consequence, the experiences we draw from golf, or any other game, are quite limited in scope and applicability. But fishing is not so much a game—or even sport—as it is an *experience* that is broad and varied in nature.

3

James P. Ignizio and Bill Ignizio

Unlike the war-and-games approach to business, fishing analogies fit the real world, allowing us to draw parallels between them and real-life situations. This, plus fishing's comfortable familiarity—even if you have never fished—make it superior as a frame of reference to war and ball games because:

- Fishing is universally understood.
- Fishing does not have a fixed time frame—like life, it just goes on.
- Fishing does not focus solely on winning or losing.
- Fishing does not diminish self-esteem—whether or not you catch anything.
- Fishing is focused on experiences, impressions, and attitudes rather than on statistics.
- Fishing involves a subtle and realistic set of rules, most of which change with time and geography.
- Fishing involves a wide assortment of gear, and encourages creativity through making and modifying equipment.
- Fishing combines survival skills (food gathering) with leisure (the act of angling).
- Fishing is played in the real world, not on a battlefield or the artificial confines of a ball field.
- Fishing emphasizes the fisherman's relationship with fish, nature, and other fishermen.
- Fishing need not take place within the confining notion of a team.
- Fishing, like business, is constantly changing.
- Fishing encourages the development of patience and persistence.
- Fishing fosters an appreciation of the natural scheme of things.
- Fishing nourishes the development of a holistic perspective, and an appreciation of those elements

of nature that serve to define the fisherman's enormous "playing field."

With fishing, unlike the war-and-games approach to business, there is no loser. Life goes on whether we catch our limit, a single fish, or nothing at all. Short-term goals, and their undue stress, are replaced by a long-term perspective, and a sense of peace. Whatever the fisherman's socioeconomic status, race, religion, gender, or politics, he or she is there not to win or lose, but to *experience* fishing.

 It takes more than a full tackle box to catch fish.

■ ■ ■

It takes (a whole lot) more than an MBA to become a successful manager.

Frank, our flustered fishing novice, has quickly discovered that quantity alone doesn't ensure success. Despite all the lures at his disposal (some fisherman call them "tools"), he was not able to catch fish. Three other critical "tools" that all good fishermen—and managers—must have are patience, persistence, and a positive attitude.

In an era of instant gratification, these three attributes are rare commodities. But this serves to make them even more valuable. Few of us are destined to find success and fortune fast, but almost all of us can—if we so choose—achieve them over the long term.

CHAPTER 2

The Old Gray Plug

After unhooking the feisty four-pound bass, the Old Angler watched as it hung suspended in the water for a few seconds before realizing it was free once again. Suddenly, with a powerful thrust of its broad tail fin, the fish disappeared into the depths.

Wiping his hands on a towel, the fisherman smiled to himself. He was unaware that his catch had been observed by anyone else. If he had known, it really wouldn't have mattered since he didn't fish to impress others.

The confident angler needs no applause.

He checked over his lure, making sure it was still in good working order. That made three bass taken from fallen trees near shore during the past hour. He hoped the pattern he had discovered would lead to at least a few more nice fish from shallow-water limbs and stumps.

Several years earlier, when the Old Angler had first taken up bass fishing, he had made a mistake he would never forget. A friend, with many years of experience in this type of fishing, had fished with him that spring day on this same reservoir.

After tossing out a variety of lures, the Old Angler fished a gray deep-diving plug off a point. After only a few turns of his reel handle, a nice bass hit the lure.

For the next two hours, his partner and he continued to work points with deep-diving plugs. His friend took five bass while the Old Angler caught none. Depositing a wriggling fish in a wire basket hung along the bow of the wooden rowboat, his partner asked him why he had quit fishing the gray plug.

"I don't know," he said. After he had caught that first fish on a gray lure, he ignored the productive color and fished just about every other hue but that one. How could he have been so stupid?

Any lure that catches fish is a good lure.

It wasn't the first mistake he had ever made and it wasn't likely to be his last. The Old Angler did, however, learn from such errors. Some fishermen, unfortunately, never seem to figure out their mistakes.

Using a foot-controlled electric motor, the white-haired fisherman headed his boat in the direction of a large fallen pine. He did not stop to work other areas that sometimes gave up a bass or two. He knew that patterns did not always hold for a prolonged period of time.

The fallen tree he targeted was a favorite of many shore fishermen. Even if he had never seen them working it, he would have known they had been there by the bobbers, rusty lures, and monofilament trimming that decorated the pine, giving it the appearance of a toppled Christmas tree, complete with ornaments.

His third cast was close to the trunk. He halted his retrieve from time to time so that the spinnerbait dropped tantalizingly down toward the lake bottom. Halfway back to the boat, a jarring strike signaled that a bass had taken the bait.

Instantly, he reeled in slack line and set the hook. The fish attempted to head back toward its woody sanctuary, but the Old Angler would have none of it. He reeled furiously, bringing the thrashing one-pounder back to the boat in short measure.

The Old Angler caught two more fish before heading to shore, both taken from woody cover and both on spinnerbaits. It had been a good day.

I'll have my tacos without *the sun-dried tomatoes*

When the Old Angler caught his four-pounder, he didn't even consider looking around to see if anyone was watching. He fishes because he likes to fish, not to impress others. In an era in which our national heroes, twenty-something ballplayers for the most part, spend more time practicing their end-zone dances than their sport, this type of self-motivation is refreshing.

....

The confident angler needs no applause.

■ ■ ■

The motivated manager doesn't need an audience.

....

In the business environment, we all too often focus our time and energy on those things that we hope will get us noticed, rather than on what we need to do—or like to do. Movies and TV would lead us to believe that we can jump from the mailroom to the boardroom if we can just find a way to get noticed. Yet it is those individuals who set their goals and do what is needed to pursue them that tend to succeed, while attention seekers continue to look for new ways to get noticed. A self-motivated person doesn't feel the need for constant attention.

The Old Angler recognizes and admits his mistakes. When he stopped using the mundane—but wildly successful—gray plug and began fishing other lures, he stopped catching fish. But he saw the error of his ways and returned to what had initially worked for him.

 Any lure that catches fish is a good lure.

■ ■ ■

Don't diversify for the sake of diversification.

A Houston restaurant owner made a similar mistake, but with much more disastrous results. This particular restaurant serves—make that used to serve—the best Tex-Mex food since the fall of the Alamo. The menu was simple and delicious, offering fantastic corn tortillas, splendid green enchiladas, mouth-watering soft and hard tacos, a fajita to die for, great salsa, the best Mexican beer, and truly extraordinary margaritas. Within a few months of opening, the restaurant's reputation had spread far and wide, with long lines of customers patiently waiting to get inside. And then, in almost the blink of an eye, they disappeared.

9

James P. Ignizio and Bill Ignizio

Why the sudden change? Well, the owner decided to "upgrade and diversify" his menu, quadrupling the items available. Lots of colorful drinks with terribly cute little umbrellas materialized. You could order everything from a seafood taco to filet mignon (with refried beans, of course). And yes, a sprinkle of sun-dried tomatoes was added to the tacos.

Aided by twenty-twenty hindsight, the reason for the restaurateur's problems seems obvious. He simply lost sight of what had made him successful to begin with. He confused more with better, fancier with tastier, and image with substance. This is pretty much the same mistake the Old Angler used when forsaking the dowdy gray plug. At least he went back to what had brought him success when his folly was pointed out to him. Our Houston restaurant owner, in contrast, blamed his woes on a fickle public rather than any shortcomings of his own. There's an old Texas saying that sums it all up: dance with the gal (or guy) who brung ya.

Bad grammar, good advice, and all too often ignored. From the small Houston restaurant to the list of Fortune 500 firms, we see people trying to be just a bit too cute. They confuse focus with narrow-mindedness. And in their hurry to get bigger, they forget just what got them there in the first place. This is not to diminish the potential of diversification. Unless you do it "right," though, it just might be best not to do it at all.

CHAPTER 3

The Better You Get,
the Luckier You Get

The "lucky" bass fisherman Frank had observed earlier slowly made his way back to the dock. Catching sight of a blue heron standing statue still in the shallows of Andrews Bay, he cut the motor to watch the patient bird do a little fishing of its own. On the bank, two Canada geese hissed at a squirrel that had wandered too close. The man enjoyed these quiet interludes every bit as much as he did fishing.

As he rested, the Old Angler reflected back on the day's trip. He had been successful largely because of the pattern he found rather early on. Patterns, he knew, played a key part in fishing.

So many fishermen, in their hurry to get "the big ones," just start toss-

11

ing out a lure or bait. They figure that successful fishing is predicated almost entirely on luck. The white-haired fishermen knew better. Successful fishing, like most things in life, is based on knowledge, experience, and a willingness to think things out carefully before jumping in.

Yes, there's some luck involved. A beginner will sometimes outcatch a fisherman with many years of experience. The Old Angler had had this happen to him a time or two. That, in his opinion, is what made fishing so much fun. You never knew what was around the next bend in the river. But he also knew that over the long haul, the skilled angler catches the most fish . . . by far.

Instead of relying on luck, the Old Angler often sought patterns when he fished. If you sat back and contemplated the situation for a while, you could generally come up with a pattern to explain why the fish held in a certain location or why they were or weren't hitting.

Find the pattern, find the fish.

The pattern he had discovered today was that the bass had snuggled up near stumps and fallen trees. Because it was a bright, sunny day, they were tucked in even tighter than usual. This meant the Old Angler's casts had to be close to cover or he would not have lured them out of hiding.

Fish, the man knew, weren't particularly bright. They were, however, blessed with instincts that served them well. In spring, they came in near shore. In hot weather, they headed back to deeper water or sought the cooling shade of weedy waters. In the fall, when the water cooled comfortably, they drifted back to the shallows. It was a predictable pattern, but only if you had taken time to figure it out.

Fishy Business

The domino effect

The Old Angler knows there are patterns to everything, although they're not always easy to find. Still, any manager worth his salt (or salmon), should be on the lookout for them. Patterns can provide clues to the causes of problems, such as the "domino effect" I encountered not so long ago.

Early one summer's morning, I received a frantic phone call from an anxious client whom I had helped install a quality-assurance program six months earlier. It had been a big success and was to be the centerpiece of the firm's next annual report. That was before things had gone terribly wrong, and product defects suddenly soared.

The manager, who assured me that they hadn't changed a thing, claimed that the situation blew up "overnight." He faxed off the most recent data, including records of daily defects for each production line.

Plotting these data against the time of day showed occurrences of higher-than-expected defects in *every* product in the plant, not just one or two. Strangely, the surge in the number of defects (indicated as vertical bars in the highly simplified diagram below) occurred twice daily for each production line (A, B, C, and D), and then the situation returned to normal. Although there was no clearly discernible pattern (see left-hand figure below), I managed to create one that resembled two sets of staircases (see right-hand figure below) by simply rearranging the plots to coincide with the plant's floor plan.

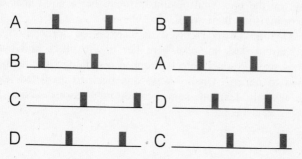

Like a long row of dominos falling, the pattern clearly revealed a wave of defects sweeping through the plant twice each day. But the cause remained a mystery.

Find the pattern, find the fish.

■　■　■

Find the pattern, solve the problem.

Taking the next plane out, I arrived at the factory with graphs and floorspace diagrams in hand. Beginning at the point where the defects started each day, I noticed that most of the assembly-line workers were male. I also observed that a young woman appeared at each point on the diagram at the same time defects seemed to peak on the charts. She would, twice daily, hand out and collect forms, and chat with the men on each production line before moving on.

The young woman, Diana, was a summer employee who was hired at precisely the time the company's quality-control program had gone "haywire." Diana was hardworking, efficient, and—through no fault of her own—quite attractive. Although she may have been unaware of the fact, her presence was quite distracting to the guys (or insensitive louts, depending on your view) on the line, who obviously found her a good deal more interesting than their work.

Domino Diana received an unexpected "promotion" the next day, a desk job that kept her in the office and out of harm's way. Product defects dropped and things ultimately returned to normal. Quality was soon back to predicted levels, and we all learned some important lessons about patterns . . . and people.

CHAPTER 4

Checking Out the Bargain Bin

B ob's Bait and Tackle is not exactly the last word in modern retailing, but it is the place to go if you're near Lake Lindner and need fishing supplies or want to rent a boat. Situated on the north shore of the two-thousand acre body of water, it's the largest of three tackle shops on the lake.

The prices aren't quite as cheap as those in most of the giant marts, and the interiors of those cavernous stores are brighter . . . and probably smell a little better, too. Still, Bob's Bait and Tackle is not hurting for business.

Bob, you see, doesn't try to attract customers; he attracts fishermen. The soda pop is cold, the bait's fresh, and ol' Bob even puts out five or six folding chairs so a tired angler can relax and talk about the big one that got away. The feel, if not the appearance, is as close to the old general store as you're likely to find nowadays.

Although Frank enjoyed soaking up the ambience of Bob's, he felt more than a little out of place. Three or four fishermen were usually there, sitting on the folding chairs or leaning against the counters and chatting. He didn't know any of them and he certainly couldn't hold his own in their conversations. (Although he had never tried.)

This was a lot different than it was at work, where Frank tended to dominate a conversation. He had the good sense, at least, to realize that this wasn't work—although he sometimes treated his new hobby precisely that way.

Frank paid the rental on the boat, and poked around a little as was becoming his custom. Maybe he could find a dandy (and worthless, of course) lure in "Bob's Bargain Bin." A purple-with-yellow-belly, red-eyed, shallow-diving crankbait caught his eye. Little wonder why that baby was in the bargain bin.

"Hey, how you doin', O.A.?" one of the fishermen called out to a late arrival.

"Just fine, Ronnie. You boys catch 'em all?"

Frank glanced over as the newcomer took a seat with the rest of the seasoned veterans. He continued rummaging through the bargain bin for that elusive winner.

"Catch anything, O.A.?"

"A couple," the man stated without embellishment.

That's when it hit Frank. The guy who had just spoken was the same fisherman he had watched reel in the whopper bass earlier that day. Lord, not only was the man an expert, he was modest on top of it. Very depressing.

For an instant, Frank considered walking over to the group and joining in the conversation. Maybe he would even introduce himself to the angler everyone called "O.A." and ask for a few bass-fishing tips.

Why not? Frank certainly wasn't shy at work; why was he so bashful here? Because he was out of his element. *Way* out. Besides, Frank hated the thought of being a novice rather than an expert.

In the meantime, Bob had wandered over to the bargain bin named in his honor and picked up a copy of a paperback book titled *Easy Guide to Bass Fishing*.

"See this?" he said to Frank. "It ain't very long and it's sure not fancy, but it's a good book if you like catchin' bass."

Good fishing can start with a good book.

Frank thanked Bob for the advice and gave the book another look. Not more than fifty pages long, it certainly wasn't slick. The copyright date was more than twenty years old. No wonder it was in the bargain bin.

Still, it was marked three dollars. Most of the lures Frank bought cost that much or more. Besides, Bob had been nice enough to show some interest ... or maybe he was just displaying a little rough-hewn sales expertise.

Whatever the case, Frank took the book to the counter and paid for it. Who knows, maybe some secret bass-fishing tactic or magical lure would be revealed in the yellowed pages of the book. Sadly, Frank had stopped believing in magic a long time ago.

Stranger in a strange land

Frank is beginning to exhibit an attribute that plays a large part in separating the successful from the unsuccessful. He wants to learn everything he can about the deceptively difficult sport of fishing. Not only does he want to learn, he actually enjoys it.

Good fishing can start with a good book.

■ ■ ■

Knowledge is the bottom line.

James P. Ignizio and Bill Ignizio

Like Frank, we are all strangers in a strange land. The last few decades have brought many changes of a more radical nature than ever before in history. We have evolved from an agricultural society to an industrial society, and now to an information-based society. Our greatest asset, in fact, is *what we know*. Never before has the old saying "knowledge is power" been more true.

Despite this, most organizations don't truly appreciate the importance of knowledge, expertise, and experience. How many firms do you know that include a line for knowledge on their balance sheet? Yet, more and more, it is a firm's knowledge base that determines its competitive stature. But, because accountants haven't learned how to put a dollar value on knowledge, it remains ignored.

It is human nature to want things to be easy; so we ignore knowledge and count bricks, blocks, equipment, and inventory—failing to realize that the only reason these "hard" assets exist is because of the collective knowledge of our organization. The story of Max and Dora graphically shows this.

Dora was the owner of an upscale women's clothing shop located at a posh seaside resort town in Northern California. Her keen eye for women's fashions and flair for window displays resulted in an overwhelmingly successful store. Despite her success, she finally tired of the grind and put the shop up for sale.

Max, an East Coast businessman, saw the shop as a real prize. One look at the books told him that Dora's place was a moneymaking machine. So, Max bought out Dora and installed one of his most trusted store managers from back east to take over.

Bad news traveled fast. Sales at the new store had dropped like a sinker in a pond. Max couldn't figure out what went wrong; but nearly every other store owner in town sure did. Max may have bought the shop, location, and existing inventory; but he didn't buy Dora's knowledge, taste, or experience. Those intangibles hadn't shown up in the books.

18

CHAPTER 5

Frank Meets the Regulars

The book wasn't what Frank had expected; it was much more. He suspected that the author, Buck Roland, may have been a talented local fisherman since many of the waters he mentioned were in the same part of the state as Lake Lindner. Whatever the case, he seemed to know his stuff.

Instead of complicating matters, the text simplified bass fishing without resorting to some of the pseudoscientific jargon found in many recently published books. Roland urged novice anglers to gain mastery of a single type of lure before going on to different baits.

Don't make fishing more complicated than it already is.

Following Roland's advice, Frank left his oversized tackle box at home that weekend and used a small one-tray box stocked with nothing but jigs of various sizes, shapes, and colors. The jig, which is no more than a weighted hook with a tail attached, was a lure Frank had trouble believing in. It just didn't look flashy enough to catch anything. Then again, nothing else had worked, so it was really no sacrifice to follow this advice.

As Roland warned, he lost a lot of lures to unseen stumps, rocks, and other hook-nabbing cover. He also caught two bass, one a keeper that weighed in the neighborhood of two pounds. He almost felt like a real bass fisherman when he entered Bob's Bait and Tackle that afternoon.

"Thanks for recommending the book," Frank said.

"Glad you liked it," Bob said, ringing up the rental fee for the boat. "Say, I think it's about time you met some of the regulars."

Why not? Frank may not have been in their league, but he felt pretty darn good about himself that day.

Mike, Chuck, and Ronnie turned out to be surprisingly pleasant company. Oh sure, there was a little bragging (they were fishermen, after all) and ribbing going on, but it was all good-natured.

"How'd you do today, Frank?" Mike asked.

"Two bass," he said proudly. "I'll be honest, that's the best I've ever done out here."

"Hey," Ronnie said, peeling the wrapper off a Twinkie, "there've been plenty a times I come back skunked altogether."

"Who hasn't?" Chuck agreed.

Who hasn't? This was a revelation to Frank. He'd always heard that fishermen exaggerate about the size and numbers of fish they caught. Seemed like these guys didn't feel the need.

It didn't take long before Frank felt at home. He didn't know if these guys were lawyers, truck drivers, salesmen, or schoolteachers. He only knew that he was enjoying himself.

When talk got around to the man everyone called O.A., Frank listened closely. The general consensus was that he was the best fisherman in that part of the state.

"This may seem like a stupid question," Frank said, "but what makes O.A. the best?"

Fishy Business

"That's simple," Ronnie answered. "He can catch just 'bout anything that swims. If the bass ain't bitin', he'll go for pike. If that don't work, he'll fish for crappies or catfish. He's got a name for it: the 'multispecies approach,' I b'lieve."

The others nodded in agreement. The Old Angler, it seemed, was far from a one-fish fisherman. Not only that, he could employ a wide variety of styles to catch specific species.

"He'll do just about anything to catch a fish," Mike agreed. "Tell him about the time he caught that pike with you."

"You guys won't let me forget that one," Chuck said.

"What happened?" Frank asked.

"Well, about two years ago this April, I guess, O.A. and me went over to Murray Lake to fish for pike. You ever catch any pike, Frank?"

"No."

"Well, Murray's got some pretty good ones, up to twelve, thirteen pounds maybe. Anyhow, O.A. and me fished big spinnerbaits all morning. Not a tap. O.A. turned to say something to me—I don't remember what—and, man, a big pike smashed his bait. He didn't even look around when he hauled back and set the hook, and I mean he set it hard."

"Tell him *how* hard," Ronnie said, chuckling.

"Well, O.A. was sitting on a portable seat I'd just bought that clamps down over the bench. Unfortunately, the clamps were a little loose. When he jerked back on the rod, the seat slid off and he sort of flew out of the boat into the lake."

"You're kidding," Frank said. "Man, I'll bet he was mad."

"He never even dropped the rod," Chuck said, shaking his head at the memory, "and he landed the pike. A nine-pounder!"

Frank joined in the laughter. O.A. was someone he had to meet.

Which books do the fish read?

Frank was fortunate to find a book that kept things simple. Whenever possible, it's wise to approach business in this way, too. Unfortunately, too many people equate "simple" with "backward."

21

Don't make fishing any more complicated than it already is.

■ ■ ■

The simplest plan is often best.

"Just-in-Time production (JIT)" is a hot idea from the recent past that contains an easily understood and reasonable concept: don't waste time and resources on the storage of inventory and raw materials that aren't yet needed. This idea appeared on the scene just as the Japanese, who had widely adopted the premise, were eating our collective lunch. The new and easy-to-understand concept worked well for them; why not for us?

Ironically, JIT began in the good ol' U.S.A. long before its adoption in Japan. Some of this nation's industrial-engineering professors taught JIT to eager students visiting from Japan who, in turn, carried the notion back to their country. Our interest in the concept was rekindled only when it reached us as an import.

JIT is just one example of the continuing reemergence of old and relatively simple concepts. In a nation that equates "old" with "inferior," we are all too prone to focus on the new (or what we think is new) and ignore the old. In doing so, we are easy prey for those who deal in hype and disguise. After all, a rose by another name just might sell for more.

Unlike so many other failed and flawed notions for productivity improvement, JIT works quite well. At least, if it is thoroughly understood and properly implemented. Undoubtedly, much of its success is due to its simplicity.

Let's examine a simple task that was *not* implemented properly: the infamous baggage-handling scheme at the new Denver airport. While this job might seem relatively straightforward, contractors for Denver's system (motivated by the demands and expectations of the airport) managed to make the procedure incredibly complex.

Fishy Business

Hordes of computers, volumes of software, masses of connections, miles and miles of wiring, and tons of sensors form the basis of this "new and improved" scheme. And it certainly contains all the elements that tend to make such concepts so attractive. It is "high-tech," "state of the art," "automated," and promises to "reduce the workforce." In short, it seemed like a surefire way to keep ahead of the pack that insists on doing their baggage handling the old-fashioned way.

Too bad it didn't work. Too bad it went *way* over budget. Too bad it went a year or so over schedule. Too, too bad.

But what happens to the manager who expresses genuine skepticism with regard to such a concept? Too often he or she is branded as old-fashioned, out of touch, and just not "with it." No wonder we sometimes allow ourselves to be swayed into accepting such new or supposedly new ideas in order to avoid being branded a corporate dinosaur.

We understand that one of the selling points of the Denver airport baggage handling system was that it was to be the equivalent of the Apollo moon-landing program. In truth, there is no comparison. The Apollo components (the Saturn launch vehicle, the Apollo module, and the support facilities) were built with tried-and-true components by means of a technology management program that could be traced back to at least World War II. The key to that program's success was a combination of simplicity and dedication—the same attributes that form the basis for success in virtually any arena.

Speaking of dedication, what about the Old Angler? And talk about concentration! The man finds himself yanked out of the boat and yet, like some amphibian version of the Energizer bunny, keeps on fishing. In a society suffering from data and information overload (we separate the two because most of the data we encounter have little or no information content), it's hard to concentrate for long on anything. It's particularly difficult to concentrate on something you don't really enjoy.

Some people may just naturally be endowed with the ability to concentrate. Even if that is the case, however, it is possible to learn how to concentrate better. Fishing is one particularly effective and pleasurable means to learn concentration.

One more observation: concentration takes practice.

23

CHAPTER 6

Make Mine Mako

While Frank continued his on-the-lake lessons with Lake Lindner's largemouth-bass population, the Old Angler had other fish to fry. The past week had not gone well for O.A., and he thought a weekend of saltwater fishing with an old friend just might clear his mind.

Following the directions Hank had supplied, O.A. turned his rental car into an oceanfront lot. Squinting out across the water, he brushed a hand through a full head of prematurely white hair. Not more than a couple of minutes later, another car pulled into the lot. A stocky figure got out and bounded over to O.A., giving him a solid bear hug.

As boys, O.A. and Hank had been as close as brothers. But for a long time now, there had been no real contact. O.A. recalled, with regret, the reason that they had lost touch, but that was all about to change now.

Draping a thick arm over O.A.'s shoulders, Hank led him down the footpath, onto the dock, and out to the boat they would be using. The sleek and powerful thirty-two-footer gleamed in the early-morning sun. It would easily make their planned fifty-mile trek in less than an hour.

Fishy Business

Onboard, Hank introduced O.A. to Manuel, the boat's owner, a short and powerfully built man in perhaps his early forties. Manuel liked O.A. almost immediately. He certainly didn't seem to be the grim and determined SOB Hank had talked about.

"Hank tells me you're quite the fisherman," Manuel said. "Maybe we can pick up a few pointers from you."

"I doubt it. Besides, I'm interested in watching you two pros at work."

You can learn a lot by just watching.

"Well, let's get at it, fellow pro," Manuel said to Hank. He flashed a puzzled smile in the direction of his friend. This was the obsessive, competitive cuss Hank had described?

Manuel shrugged it off. He had learned long ago that many things change over the years. Besides, none of that really mattered now; it was time to go fishing.

As promised, Manuel brought the threesome to "the spot" somewhere off San Clemente Island well before sunrise. The men could hear the bark of the sea lions and the splashes they made as they slid awkwardly off the rocks into the water. Hank handed O.A. a cup of coffee and told him to relax while he and Manuel ran through  a final check of their gear. O.A. might not have ever fished for mako, but he had certainly read a lot about them. Here, off the Southern California coast, the shortfin makos—mostly juveniles weighing somewhere between thirty and a hundred and fifty pounds—start making their appearance in early July.

O.A. volunteered to pilot, and held the boat's speed at roughly six knots. Although Hank and Manuel both used trolling rods with lever-drag reels, each fished different plugs. If action was not forthcoming, they would not hesitate to change colors.

If the lures didn't work, Manuel would switch to the backup—live mackerel on downriggers and outriggers. O.A. never ceased to be amazed by the complexity and ingenuity of the seemingly simple sport of fishing. When he first got seriously involved in it, he had wondered just how long something so "simple" would hold his attention.

The more he fished, the more he came to appreciate how much he didn't know—and probably never would. Whether it was on Lake Lindner or the most remote trout stream, fishing had a way of making you think in a manner unlike anything else O.A. had encountered.

Before he had a chance to ponder this philosophical issue further, O.A. noticed the upward flash of something big becoming airborne. The fish hit the water and stripped off a good hundred yards of line before it registered on O.A. that the first mako, a ninety-pound beauty, had been hooked.

Two makos later, Manuel prodded O.A. to try his hand at the sport. He was overjoyed at hauling in a thrashing ninety-five-pounder followed by a feisty sixty-pound specimen. By day's end, the three men had combined for a total of seven makos, ranging in size from forty to a hundred and ten pounds.

The fish were quickly tagged and released. The exhausted but delighted fishermen relived the battles as they headed back. For O.A., the trip had been just what the doctor ordered.

The more you learn, the more there is to learn

Although the boys back at Bob's Bait and Tackle see O.A. as a happy-go-lucky guy, he has worries of his own. The mako-fishing jaunt was his way of pondering and hopefully solving his private problems.

Years ago things would have been different. O.A. would most likely have made some sort of a decision in a flash and

Fishy Business

followed through . . . relentlessly. But years of fishing—as well as life in general—had taught him a number of lessons. Some hard, some easy. Whether fishing with a cane pole off a river-bank, casting from his fourteen-foot rowboat, working a dry fly for trout, or pursuing mako, things were seldom as they seemed. Besides, the fastest way to scare fish is to make a lot of noise or a quick movement.

O.A.'s boyhood buddy Hank noticed a change in his once-brash friend. Had O.A. gone soft?

You can learn a lot by just watching.

■ ■ ■

Take the time to observe.

O.A. exhibited another characteristic Hank may have found odd, at least in our culture. He made the conscious decision to watch the other two men fish for mako for some time before trying it himself. Despite the years of fishing experience for a host of different species by a variety of approaches, O.A. still recognizes just how little he really knows about fishing. But don't be misled, he is not afraid of making a mistake; he just wants to gain an understanding and appreciation of what it takes to fish for mako before trying it himself.

It might be wise to follow O.A.'s lead. Before taking on something new and different, find out how others have han-dled the situation. The smart manager knows that there is much to learn through observation. The following is a case in point.

One of the world's biggest oil refineries had a policy with production schedulers that needlessly cost them millions of dol-lars. These schedulers, who determine when to start and end production runs, must be constantly aware of customer deliv-ery dates as well as the status of the entire refinery.

James P. Ignizio and Bill Ignizio

The policy was to bring in a new scheduler every two or three years, rotating them from one job to another as they progressed through the ranks. The new job, generally at some other location, meant that like ships in the night, the two individuals would pass without an exchange of greeting—or information.

Top management never caught on that the policy forced the incoming scheduler to learn the new job from scratch without the benefit of working with the previous scheduler. The practice meant that the refinery's costs rose dramatically with the appointment of each new scheduler. Deliveries were late, the wrong products were produced, and the wrong mixes were scheduled.

It usually took a year or so before the new scheduler was finally up to speed. About the time he or she really started cooking, another rotation of personnel occurred. The costs associated with the flawed policy were on the order of five to ten million dollars a year. If top management had taken the time to observe what was happening, the problem could have easily been avoided by simply overlapping the assignments of the new and old scheduler.

28

CHAPTER 7

Ellen's a Good Sport

Ellen looked at the small bottle filled with colorful jelly beans and smiled. The label read: DR. FISHGOOD'S PRE-SCRIPTION FOR FISHIN'—*Stomachache? Tension? Bad breath? Well, forget about these pills and* GO FISHIN'! IT'S GOOD FOR WHAT AILS YOU!

So far, at least, fishing had certainly been good for Frank. He was, by his own admission, no angling superstar; nevertheless, he generally enjoyed his outings on Lake Lindner each weekend. Not every day went smoothly, of course. There was, for instance, one memorable outburst when he punted his tackle box the length of the driveway after yet another unsuccessful outing. Thankfully, Ellen had not witnessed that little stunt, although she did notice the large dent in his new box.

Despite such setbacks, Frank had made some new (low-stress, thankfully) friends and seemed to have forgotten about golf. This pleased Ellen no end. Although she was the culprit who had introduced him to the game, he never really took to it the way she had hoped. Oh sure, he played it a lot. But instead of relaxing on the course, he just became more tense.

She was afraid, at first, that fishing might turn out the same way. While there was no score to keep, Frank had the uncanny knack of turning virtually any activity into a competitive event. As far as Ellen could tell, that hadn't happened with fishing. She hoped it would last.

The successful fisherman isn't necessarily the one who catches the most fish.

Frank had been after Ellen for a long time to join him on the waters of beautiful (he assured her) Lake Lindner. She had finally agreed, although the idea of sitting cramped up in a little boat for three or four hours really didn't appeal to her. Still, she didn't want to dampen Frank's enthusiasm.

Getting up at five in the morning—on Saturday, no less—was something she didn't think she would ever get used to. Frank, happy as a clam or carp (or whatever lived in Lake Lindner), was already downstairs loading the car.

"You're gonna love it, Ellen," he said, turning off the main highway onto the gravel road that led to Bob's Bait and Tackle.

Well, Frank loved it and that was good enough for her. He piloted the car through a thick stand of pines before the lake came into view. A feathery mist wisped off the water's surface as a small cluster of mallards poked about the aquatic weeds for . . . well, for whatever it is that mallards poke around for.

As her eyes adjusted to the dim light, Ellen made out the silhouette of a fisherman anchored down near the mouth of a small bay. Frank ushered her into the bait shop, where he introduced her to Bob.

"Bluegills are hittin'," Bob said casually.

"Ellen and I are going for bass," Frank explained.

"What a surprise. Still, there's some nice bluegills out there. Sure you don't want some maggots?"

If Ellen wasn't totally awake by now, that statement did the trick. "Did you say maggots?"

Fishy Business

"Uh-huh." Bob had seen the reaction plenty of times, but he never failed to enjoy the impact of the word on novices.

"I don't think we'll need any maggots," Frank said. In truth, the idea of attempting to impale a squirmy little maggot on a hook didn't much appeal to him.

"What the heck," Ellen said, surprising them both, "let's have some maggots."

A maggot to you is a feast to a bluegill.

"Got bobbers?" Bob asked, pulling a small container of maggots out of a grimy old refrigerator.

"Sure," Frank said, warily eyeing the cup of maggots.

Bob then did something Frank hadn't expected: he shook the container gently, as if to wake up the little guys. Next he opened the lid to display the bait, which was wriggling about in what appeared to be a fine bedding of sawdust.

Ellen didn't know whether to laugh or scream. But Bob wasn't through yet. He nonchalantly tipped the cup into his hand to display the bait. Frank tried to appear calm.

"Anything else?" Bob asked, pouring the lively maggots back into the cup and snapping the lid on.

"Don't think I could handle anything else right now," Frank said. "Let's go pick out a boat."

You're going to work, not war!

Although Frank is happier with his latest hobby than he thought possible, he still has a long way to go. He insists on bass fishing almost exclusively, and meticulously keeps a log of the number, length, and approximate weight of fish he catches on each outing.

The successful fisherman isn't necessarily the one who catches the most fish.

■ ■ ■

Don't confuse obsession with competitiveness.

It's difficult for him to overcome his highly competitive nature and simply go with the flow. At work, his management style still more closely resembles that of ball games or war. After all, he has been well taught that the axioms below are not to be questioned:

- Every problem is a competition; it's always "us" against "them."
- Every team needs a star player.
- Every problem, like every opponent, must be defeated.
- If a player doesn't perform, it's back to the minor leagues—or worse.
- Instead of looking into the future, each player is obsessed with his or her current statistics.
- Every problem is viewed as a game with a limited number of innings (or periods, or quarters, or ammunition).
- Just as every game has its hero, it also has its goat. And aren't we *all* scared to death of being the goat?
- You have to fight to win.
- You *have* to win.

Fishy Business

It may take a while, but we suspect that Frank is on his way to discovering that business need not always be this way. A less combative approach can actually sharpen a person's analytical skills and make decision making more effective. This doesn't mean that you aren't competitive, just that you choose to channel your time and energies toward objectives that ultimately pay off.

Frank is still grappling with this notion, and you can hardly blame him. It goes against most of what he was taught in business school and his own personal experiences. If he had adopted this philosophy in college, he's certain he never would have won the hard-fought battle for the number-two spot on the tennis team.

His company leaders certainly don't endorse a "wimpy" management style. Just a few months ago, they implemented a weekend course in "action management" similar to those initiated by British firms in the mid-nineties.

Frank's "platoon," led by his immediate superior at work, "Big Jake," marched into the experience with great expectations. The company CEO emphatically stated that the course would instill the troops with a fighting spirit and lead them all to glorious victory. He didn't mention that it was also designed to break those weak-willed employees who might better serve the firm by resigning.

Big Jake, who insisted that his underlings call him "Colonel" during the exercise, barked orders from the comfort of the sidelines. Even the toughest Marine Corps drill sergeant would have admired the constant train of insults he heaped upon the hapless troops.

Frank, still in good shape from his college tennis days, considered the course as yet another chance to prove himself. Walter, a pudgy, bright, cheerful, and easygoing guy in accounting, found it memorable, to say the least. After suffering hypothermia and a fractured left arm (there are, after all, casualties in war), he landed in the hospital. There, as a matter of fact, was where Big Jake sent him his termination notice.

Frank wasn't nearly as proud as he thought he'd be at the graduation ceremonies held in the company cafeteria the following week. Rather than building morale and team spirit, the course had left many of the participants with a festering residue of anger and humiliation. More than one of the troops complained about the insensitivity and injustice of Walter's "dishonorable discharge."

Frank was beginning to wonder if rappelling from cliffs, building makeshift rafts, blowing up dinghies, and navigating icy waters really helped improve the way managers functioned at work, but he kept his mouth shut. He couldn't risk being mustered out.

Speaking of "risks," let's return to the matter of maggots for a moment. Both Ellen and Frank weren't in any big hurry to fish with the things. They had been taught since youth that these baby bugs are among the most despised creatures on earth. No wonder they didn't just pop open the maggot container's lid and grab a couple of the wiggly insect larvae. Bluegills, however, find them particularly appetizing. And after all is said and done, that's what really matters.

 A maggot to you is a feast for a bluegill.

■ ■ ■

Give the customer what he wants.

CHAPTER 8

You're Going to Put What on the Hook?

Although the weather cooperated nicely, the bass did not. Ellen took it all in stride, but she was beginning to suspect that her earlier hunch was right. Fishing was pretty boring.

"Want to try for some bluegills?" Frank asked after two hours of bassless fishing.

"Sure," she said gamely. How could it be any worse?

Frank anchored down near a cluster of lily pads and both he and Ellen tied on the small weighted hooks Bob called panfish spoons. Frank positioned their bobbers about two feet above the hook (why not?) and opened the maggot container. If his wife hadn't been there, he probably would have dumped the disgusting creatures into the water and forgotten about bluegill fishing altogether.

"Frank," Ellen said, "have you done this before? I mean, have you ever used maggots?"

"No," Frank admitted, looking her in the eye.

They stared at each other for a few seconds before realizing that each was trying to forestall the moment of truth when they would have to grab and hook a maggot. Finally, Ellen could stand it no longer and broke into spasms of laughter. Maybe fishing was fun after all.

"Look," Frank said, trying to get serious again, "if we want to catch bluegills, we're going to have to get the stupid things on the hook."

"Got any Super Glue?" Ellen deadpanned. "You go first, O mighty fisherman." A challenge. Ellen knew instinctively that Frank would rise to the bait, so to speak. And he did. It wasn't a pretty sight, with neither the maggot nor Frank faring too well. Finally, though, he triumphed with a secured, although somewhat worse-for-wear bait. Not wishing to be outdone, Ellen pulled out a wiggling maggot of her own and, after a few errant tries, hooked it.

"And you truly enjoy this?" she said, casting out.

"Love it!" Frank answered.

After twenty minutes of maggot dunking, Frank began to suspect that the bluegills were off somewhere socializing with the bass. The maggot caper had brightened Ellen's spirits, but things were beginning to slow down again.

Although Frank hid it well, he was smoldering inside. It was the way he felt after hitting an errant tee shot: he no longer had control over the situation. At times like this, fishing didn't seem very relaxing.

"Hey, Frank—how ya' doin'?" It was Ronnie. They hadn't noticed his boat cruising in their direction until he called out.

Frank handled the introductions and Ronnie was gracious in his homespun way. He chatted about what a great day it was to be on the lake and how conditions were absolutely "ideal" for fishing.

"I gotta tell you," Ronnie said. "I'm surprised to see y'all fishin' for 'gills. I thought you was exclusively a bass fisherman."

"Well, to tell you the truth, we're not doing so well with either species," Frank revealed.

"How far down's your bait?" Ronnie asked.

"About two, maybe three, feet below the bobber," Frank said.

"Try six or seven," Ronnie suggested before moving off. "Nice meetin' you, Ellen."

Fish can be picky.

Since they hadn't caught anything up to now, Frank decided to follow Ronnie's advice. Almost immediately, his bobber dipped down and he reeled in a chunky bluegill. Within an hour, they had two dozen fat bluegills in the fish basket.

During the ride home, Frank imagined the glorious fish fry they would feast on that evening. Why hadn't he tried bluegill fishing before?

"Frank." Ellen interrupted his thoughts. "How did Ronnie know we'd catch those fish by just lowering the bait?"

"I don't really know," Frank said, but he was determined to find out.

Excuse me, where's the rest room?

Frank thought he was doing everything right. Since the bluegills were hitting, he agreed to fish for them instead of his beloved bass. He took Bob's expert advice on bait, even though he wasn't too thrilled about the selection. Frank and Ellen were in the right place, with the right bait, at the right time—and they *still* couldn't catch fish. Then along comes Ronnie, a seemingly uncomplicated fellow with an even more uncomplicated idea: just lower the bait.

Fish can be picky.

■ ■ ■

In business, every detail matters.

When working on the Apollo moon-landing program, I encountered a similar situation in which a small detail made a huge difference. Once the second stage of the Saturn rocket (the booster for the Apollo) reached Cape Kennedy, we found that our telemetry transmitters didn't work. This made no sense. We had tested them in California before and after installation. We then transported the stage to Mississippi and tested the transmitters again. In every instance they worked fine. But at Cape Kennedy, they failed at an alarming rate. It was baffling.

Our technicians noticed only one thing even the slightest bit unusual: there seemed to be some faint stains on the failed transmitters' cases, at the points where they fastened to the instrumentation panels. From a technical perspective, this ruined their grounding. The company brought in some heavy-duty (read: expensive) consultants. They were clueless. Those of us who had spent a fair amount of time at the Mississippi facility, however, were able to put two and two together.

The Saturn rocket was placed upright at the Mississippi test site and put through its paces. The technicians and engineers who conducted some of these tests took an elevator to the top of the booster. You could enter the instrumentation area only if you had on a "clean suit" and plastic "booties." It was a slow ride up, and just as slow back down. If nature called, you had to leave the stage, remove your protective clothing, take the elevator down, and make a long, uncomfortable walk to the rest room. Some innovative folks found a faster way. When no one was looking, they simply relieved themselves inside the booster, and sometimes on the telemetry transmitters.

Like Frank in his quest for bluegills, we thought we had done everything right. We certainly did it "according to the book." But our book didn't mention anything about the importance of the location of rest rooms.

CHAPTER 9

Ronnie's a Deep Fisher

The next time Frank ran into Ronnie, he asked how he knew at precisely what depth the bluegills were holding on the day he and Ellen had fished Lake Lindner. Ronnie cryptically answered that he had seen the fish on his "machine."

"If you want, we'll go out sometime and I'll show you how it works."

Frank thanked Ronnie for the offer. He wanted very much to learn more about this remarkable machine.

The next weekend, Frank joined Ronnie on the water. It was the first time he had fished with one of the "regulars" (as he had come to think of the Bait Shop Gang). The outing reinforced the fact that he had plenty to learn.

The machine Ronnie had referred to was a depth finder, as Frank suspected. He had seen and read about them, although he had never used one. He also noted that all the TV fishermen had one, and sometimes two, mounted on their fancy bass boats.

"See them dots." Ronnie pointed at pixels on the depth finder's screen. "That's a school a small fish smack dab under the boat. The scale here says they're holdin' in 'bout ten feet a water."

Fishy Business

Frank was impressed. "Man, that's so easy, it's almost like cheating."

"I wish," Ronnie said, with a wry smile. "Say, look at them big fish on the screen there."

"What are they?" Frank asked.

"Well, I can't rightly say, but they could be bass swimmin' 'round in twelve feet a water. Got any ideas how to catch 'em?"

"Jigs?" Frank hazarded.

"Why not?" Ronnie agreed, tying on a jig.

From what Frank could figure out, he and Ronnie were practically dropping the lead-weighted lures right on top of the bass. But it didn't seem to interest the fish. Next they cast out crankbaits, plastic worms, and jigging spoons. Those lures also failed.

"Still feel like we're cheatin'?" Ronnie asked.

A depth finder won't catch fish for you.

"Well, I guess they're just not hitting today," Frank said. He found it difficult to understand how Ronnie could take their failure so calmly. Didn't *anything* upset the guy?

"Let's troll a little bit with crankbaits before we head back," Ronnie suggested.

After forty minutes of dragging their lures behind the boat at various speeds and using different trolling patterns, Frank was getting antsy. Why didn't the impossibly patient ol' Ronnie see that it was hopeless? That's when the bass hit his plug.

"Got one!" he grunted, setting the hook.

Ronnie cut the motor and reeled in his lure to give his partner some "fightin' room." At first, Frank thought he had hooked a big catfish. It was certainly larger than any bass he had ever had on the end of his line.

Several minutes later, the blurry image of a big fish could be seen beneath the water's rippling surface. It was a bass, and

41

a big one. Frank was so excited, he made a couple of what could have been critical mistakes. Fate was smiling, however, and he maneuvered a six-pound largemouth into Ronnie's waiting net.

This fish would be kept for the wall. Ronnie shook Frank's hand and they headed back to shore. Frank fervently hoped some of the boys were still at Bob's. A little bragging was in order.

On the way in, Ronnie told him how depth finders had changed over the years from simple round-faced flashers to the more advanced units such as the one he owned. Some even scanned the lake bottom off to the sides as well as directly below the transducer.

"It takes some learnin', but these things really help when you understand how to use 'em," Ronnie said. "Tell you the truth, fishin' without one is kinda like fishin' blindfolded. You can do it, but why would you want to?"

If Frank hadn't already known it, this day proved that knowing where the fish were was only part of the equation. You also had to unlock the secret of catching them. It was Ronnie's experience that brought him a trophy that day.

He wondered out loud if he would ever grasp all the intricacies of this "simple" hobby.

"You will," Ronnie said, "but you just gotta do it one little bit at a time, that's all."

Would you type this for me?

There may be more to ol' Ronnie than meets the eye. He's certainly up to date on the latest high-tech fishing tools; he also knows it takes more than high tech to catch fish.

A depth finder won't catch fish for you.

■ ■ ■

People make technology work.

Fishy Business

With all the hype about the global information highway, smart cars, intelligent roadways, and automated factories, you might assume that humans won't have much to do except baby-sit a bunch of robots and "smart" machines. You'd be wrong.

We have a long, long way to go before we're all replaced by machines. High tech has brought about changes, certainly, but people must decide how these changes are implemented. A decade or so ago, the newly minted MBA could, in most instances, function effectively without much understanding of technology. Although personal computers were on just about everyone's desk, very few people really knew what to do with them.

An example: one firm spent a great deal of money to re-train their secretaries. Having thrown away all their IBM Selectric typewriters, management replaced them with personal computers and word-processing software. All that was needed, they figured, was to train the secretaries to "type" on the computers—and it would be business as usual.

The management at this company pictured the computer as a high-tech substitute for a typewriter. That kind of thinking may have worked fine when manual typewriters were replaced by electric models, but the analogy simply didn't hold for the transition from typewriter to computer.

Computers ended up on the desks of everyone, not just the secretaries. Instead of handing a letter or report to be typed up by a secretary, many of the white-collar workers did it themselves. Not only that, they were able to save a copy on the computer disk, and run spell checks and grammar checks on each document. It wasn't long before the retrained secretaries found themselves with less and less to type, and of less value to the organization.

The computer not only changed the manner in which secretaries typed, it virtually eliminated their traditional place in the organization. Instead of training the secretaries to type with a word processor, they should have been trained in such areas as the use of databases to collect and maintain company records. It is obvious that we need to be creative to get the most out of high tech. We must also anticipate the impact.

James P. Ignizio and Bill Ignizio

Here's a quick look at another example of the creative implementation of high technology in the form of a riddle. See if you can solve it. The Japanese did.

If you've ever seen a chemical processing plant, you know that they all look pretty much the same, with lots of vats and containers and lots and lots of pipes leading from one container to another. To get the feel of it all, just imagine yourself in a huge room with a king-size chemistry set.

To process chemicals, you must mix them in certain containers and then pipe them to others. Whenever a new "recipe" is called for, those nasty pipes must be laboriously rearranged. For decades, that's the way things have been done. How do you think one Japanese firm improved upon the method? We'll reveal the answer in the next chapter.

CHAPTER 10

That Bass Has Whiskers!

With a little help from Ronnie and Bob, Frank purchased an inexpensive depth finder of his own. While it was not as high-tech as Ronnie's, both men assured him it would do the job.

It didn't. While Frank found the depth finder easy enough to operate, he was unable to catch fish. This particular problem was becoming all too familiar. Much like work, Frank was developing a love-hate relationship with fishing. At times, both pursuits could be quite fulfilling. On other occasions, they simply ticked him off.

Renting a boat and electric motor from Bob, he trolled the same type of lure that had worked so well the previous Saturday. He even fished the same area.

After two hours, he motored over to a submerged island and began working a jig. He was still jigging the structure twenty minutes later when he spotted the Old Angler. With two rods positioned in holders on each side of the boat, the white-haired fisherman's attention was riveted on his depth finder.

As Frank watched, O.A. suddenly grabbed the inside rod. The pronounced bend in the rod announced the presence of a big fish.

Frank reeled in his lure and watched the show. This was the second time he had witnessed O.A. in action.

This time, however, was different from the first. The fish did not come in nearly as quickly as the bass he saw him catch several weeks ago. O.A. was apparently unconcerned, though, and seemed to have everything under control.

At any moment now, Frank expected to see the fish explode on the surface, spraying water in all directions. It didn't happen. O.A., moving out from shore to prevent the fish tangling his line and breaking off, continued the fight in open water.

Several seconds later, he reached for the net (which he had placed on the seat next to him earlier) and scooped up a huge fish. Next he grabbed a pair of pliers and unhooked the behemoth. As he was dislodging the hook, he noticed Frank for the first time. He motioned him over.

The organized angler loses fewer fish.

The catch was a channel catfish O.A. estimated to weigh in at about ten or eleven pounds. Frank shook his head at the size of the bewhiskered beast.

"You caught that on a lure?" he asked. "I thought catfish only ate live bait."

"Oh, they eat dead bait, too," O.A. said, smiling. "They also hit lures sometimes."

After talking for a while, the two fishermen went off in different directions. O.A. continued trolling parallel to shore and Frank returned to jigging the hump he had been working earlier.

He refused to be discouraged. There was a lot to learn,

sure, but he was determined to educate himself. For starters, he would reread the book he bought several weeks earlier at Bob's. He also thought it might be a good idea to see what the library had to offer on the subject of trolling.

The long winter ahead would provide plenty of time for study.

Some people spend half their lives just looking for their keys!

The Old Angler has been fishing long enough to realize just how important it is to be both organized and prepared. Books can help, certainly, but there's no substitute for experience. Frank, who seems to be a lot more patient than when we first met him, is beginning to see this. He doesn't get discouraged nearly as quickly as before, and has already learned enough about fishing to recognize how much more he needs to learn.

 The organized angler loses fewer fish.

■ ■ ■

It's hard to run an organization unless you're organized.

We've all met managers, sometimes even successful ones, whose desks and offices look like the aftermath of a bad train wreck. Papers, books, documents, and unopened correspondence are spread everywhere. Such people even defend their messes with this well-known rationalization: "An organized desk is the sign of a closed mind."

While they may want desperately to believe this myth, the fact is that these disorganized types waste enormous amounts of time just looking for the "right information." As for making

James P. Ignizio and Bill Ignizio

decisions, our schools spend little time on the art and science of organization and orderliness. In fact, this topic is often ridiculed. It's as though these skills might discourage free thinking. That's too bad because organization and self-discipline can work wonders.

Oh, yes—we haven't forgotten the riddle posed about chemical plants in the previous chapter. Have you figured out how the Japanese company improved the transfer of chemicals from one container to the other?

Instead of thinking about how chemical processing plants *now* function, they thought about how they *should* function. The Japanese approached the problem from an entirely different perspective, creating a plant without the familiar maze of pipes. Instead of moving chemicals from one container to another via pipes, it's the *containers* that move.

When the contents of one container need to be transferred to another, the robot containers actually meet each other on the plant floor. A small pipe from one extends to the receptacle on the other. Once the contents have been transferred, the pipe retracts, and the neatly choreographed robot ballet continues. Whenever they need to change the "recipe," they just change the "dance."

The solution is unique, to say the least. If you were to draw an analogy to fishing, it would be as remarkable as finding a way to fish without a line.

CHAPTER 11

Perfect Timing

Something was wrong with the office clock. Time has a way of crawling, Frank discovered, when you've got a big date with some hungry bass. Ronnie had called the night before, informing him that this was it: the bass were on the prowl. Would Frank like to accompany him? He didn't have to ask twice.

When five o'clock finally arrived, Frank took off before Big Jake even realized he had left the building. Despite the long hours and weekends he put in at work, he knew that Jake would never condone such time-wasting foolishness as fishing. At the moment, Frank really didn't give a catfish's whisker about Jake's views on the subject. Within fifteen minutes of leaving the office, he was at the lake.

"Right on time, ol' buddy," Ronnie said, loading his rods into the boat. "Ready to go?"

"Absolutely," Frank said. "You think they're still hitting?"

"They were hittin' yesterday," Ronnie said.

"But that doesn't mean they'll be hitting today, does it?"

"Nothin' in life's absolutely for certain, Frank. Still, I think we got a real good chance of catchin' a few."

"Tell me, Ronnie—how in the world can a person predict with any certainty when bass are going to hit?"

"Like I said, you can't always. But bass cruise the shallows lookin' for food in the early fall. This is early fall, and them bass are cruisin'," Ronnie said.

"Now, if we'd have gone out last week, forget it. A cold front passed through and turned 'em off. Today, all systems are go, Frank."

Successful fishermen know when—as well as how—to fish.

Ronnie's prediction proved accurate. He took four bass that day while Frank managed to bring in three, all keepers. It was the most bass he had ever caught in a single day.

Too soon? Too late? Too bad.

The most sorrowful words a fisherman is likely to hear are: "You should have been here last week." Lucky Frank. The week he and Ronnie chose to go fishing was the week "you should have been here." Too bad things don't always work out that well.

Two common reasons for having a great business idea fail are "being on the lake" a little too soon or a little too late. You might come up with a terrific plan; but if it's not implemented at just the right time, you may find that you've lost an opportunity that won't come around again.

50

Successful fishermen know when—
as well as how—to fish.

■　■　■

Timing is critical.

Ted and Marvin, two young hires at a major consulting firm, illustrate this point. Ted, who told us the tale, is bright, creative, and highly impatient. When an idea strikes him, he can't wait to get at it. Marvin, on the other hand, is slower to act. He makes up for this shortcoming with an uncanny sense of timing . . . and a regrettable lack of conscience.

Sometime back, the boys' boss, Roger, was in the throes of a really lousy week. A few days earlier, he had lost a bitter custody case for his young son. A fender bender on the way to work that morning topped it all off. When he finally arrived at the office, wondering what the damage to his spanking-new BMW would run, Ted was waiting to pounce on him with a fabulous idea.

Roger half listened while Ted excitedly explained his latest concept: a plan for improving the firm's proprietary approach to information processing. As Ted rambled on, Roger's thoughts turned to the disappointments and mishaps of the last several days. It wasn't too surprising that he forgot all about Ted's idea the moment the younger man left his office.

Ted, bitterly disappointed at Roger's reaction (or lack thereof), shared his idea with Marvin. Marvin, who knew a marvelous concept when he heard one, waited patiently for a week or so until Roger mellowed out.

He spent the intervening time polishing Ted's idea to a fine luster. Then, at just the right time, he tossed the concept in Roger's direction. Roger caught it and loved it, of course. Such originality was rare, indeed.

Ted was miffed, but he learned a great deal about timing from his ex-buddy Marvin.

CHAPTER 12

Long John and the Bass Barrel

It had been an uncharacteristically mild November. The regulars at Bob's Bait and Tackle didn't mind, and spent every spare minute they could on the water. But Big Jake had kept Frank so busy he was able to fish the lake only once that month.

Several times after work, however, he got in some casting practice in his backyard. The satisfying clang of an on-target toss as it hit the garbage-can lid—placed forty feet away—was becoming more common.

As temperatures cooled drastically, only the most ardent diehards ventured onto the lake. Frank put his gear away, but continued to read whatever he could on fishing. With forecasters calling for Saturday's temperatures to be in the high twenties, he was surprised when Ronnie called Friday night.

"I'm not callin' to go fishin'," Ronnie explained. "You interested in goin' to the big sports show with Mike and me tomorrow?"

Ronnie made it sound tempting. There would be endless aisles of the latest fishing gear and seminars on the hour by expert anglers, including a couple of TV fishermen.

Fishy Business

The next morning, Ronnie picked up Frank and along with Mike they set off for the sports show. On display were boats, fish finders, lures, rods and reels of all descriptions, and even a huge fish tank called the "Bass Barrel."

Experts would climb up a ladder to the top of the oversized aquarium where the bow of a bass boat had been mounted. From that precarious perch they would lecture the audience on the finer points of fishing.

The first speaker, John Short (nicknamed "Long John," of course), was largely ignored by Frank, who kept staring at the fish. Finally, a friendly nudge from Ronnie snapped him out of his daze.

"You heard anything ol' John up there's said?" Ronnie whispered.

"Something about spinnerbaits, I think," Frank answered.

"Better listen," Mike said. "There'll be a quiz later."

A good fisherman should listen.

Frank tried to tune in to Long John's message, but the fascination of watching live bass swimming around in front of him proved a powerful attraction. He was not alone. The highlight of the seminar, judging from the reaction of the crowd, came when one of the Bass Barrel largemouths nabbed a spinnerbait.

It happened so quickly Frank almost missed it. The fish was cruising lazily near the bottom of the tank when it opened its jaws, as though yawning, and the lure simply disappeared inside that cavernous mouth.

John, who was looking out at the audience and discussing lure color at the time, instinctively jerked back on the rod and the fight was on. Frank was mesmerized by the underwater struggle. Then the big bass opened its mouth and the spinnerbait fell out.

53

"No hook point," John explained as the crowd applauded appreciatively.

Frank may have missed most of Long John's lecture, but that lightning-quick hookset taught him a lesson he would remember for a long time.

What did you say?

Whether they know it or not, the MTV generation is at a disadvantage when it comes to business. Flashy presentations, with plenty of color and noise, make it difficult to concentrate on what's important. But TV isn't the only problem. Listening is hard!

To compound the difficulty, we too often make listening even harder than it needs to be. Distractions can turn listening into grueling work. Frank, whose attention was drawn to the bass tank, missed out on most of what the fishing expert said.

A good fisherman should listen.

■ ■ ■

A good manager listens.

Some insist that making things more interesting encourages people to listen. In many cases that's absolutely true, but it can be overdone. One of the most popular professors at a major university rarely failed to please his audience. When lecturing on Napoleon, he came to class dressed like the little general. When he covered the migration of the Acadians from Canada to Louisiana, he brought steamed crawfish to class—and invited each student to partake of the Cajun delicacy. He won a wallful of teaching awards, and his classes were always packed.

When a number of former students were interviewed five years or so after graduation, they recounted with astonishing

Fishy Business

accuracy most of the professor's performances—down to such minutiae as the number of feathers in Yankee Doodle's hat. But when it came to remembering history, they were pretty much at a loss. No matter, they still thought that the ol' professor was one heck of a teacher.

We're certainly not advocating that a lecture or book has to be deadly dull to convey its teachings. But entertainment can get in the way of the message. The professor's act, well-meaning as it was, distracted his students' attention away from the lesson he was trying so hard to convey.

Although difficult, the students needed to concentrate on his words rather than his antics. Many simply couldn't. In today's world, distractions are everywhere. The successful individual is the one who finds a way to shut out these distractions and *listen*.

CHAPTER 13

The Scarlet Lure

A chill was in the air as Frank drove to the lake to return a book on depth finders that Ronnie had loaned him. As he approached the bait shop, Frank noticed Chuck sitting at one of the outdoor picnic benches, absorbed in some early-morning project. He had several tackle boxes on the table, a green garbage bag at his feet, and two growing piles of fishing paraphernalia, mostly lures, laid out before him.

"Morning, Chuck, Doing some fall cleaning?"

"Hi, Frank. Yup, taking out the trash."

Frank looked closely at the two piles and was a bit perplexed to discover that there seemed to be a mixture of old and new, junk and treasure, in each. "Which pile are you throwing away?" Frank asked, eyeing a particularly attractive and nearly new flashy red crankbait.

"The one on the right's the good stack. The stuff on the left is going to that big tackle box in the sky, I'm afraid."

"Mind if I grab that little red lure before it passes on?"

"Not at all, but why do you want it?"

"It looks practically brand-new, Chuck. I think quite a few

56

bass will chase after that scarlet devil," Frank said, attempting a rather lame Clark-Gable-as-Rhett-Butler impersonation.

"Well, you're welcome to it, but I've never caught anything with it, Frank. Now, see this baby?" Chuck said, pointing to a chipped gray plug.

"They don't make these plugs anymore. O.A. gave me this one years ago. Believe me, it works."

"And the red one doesn't?" Frank couldn't believe it.

"Not for me, but you take it and see if it works for you," Chuck said, handing Frank the glitzy red model.

A well-stocked tackle box has the right combination of new and old.

Frank thanked Chuck for the lure, not realizing that he would soon learn that Chuck was right. New doesn't always mean better. Neither does flashy. Seems like some lures attract more fishermen than fish.

There's more than one way to improve the bottom line

About two weeks after Frank had observed Chuck tidying up his gear, an important meeting took place at work. Frank, who took his customary seat next to Big Jake, saw that the conference room was packed.

The gaggle of consultants marched in, single file, reminding Frank of a bunch of toy soldiers in business suits. He certainly didn't think of himself as old, but he was taken aback by their bright young faces. He doubted if any of the "troops" was more than two or three years out of business school.

Their spokesperson's findings were no surprise. It was precisely the same message they had delivered to every previous client. The company had to downsize if it was to remain competitive. This meant getting rid of the "high-priced help." And for this, they charged Frank's company nearly a half million.

Big Jake actually applauded at the end of the presentation. Ever since being hired as VP of manufacturing less than a year ago, Jake had argued for a workforce reduction. He had been so convincing that Frank found himself agreeing with the idea.

It wasn't long before Frank became one of the firm's most enthusiastic supporters of downsizing. Everyone else on the planet was downsizing, why not them? Here, he had thought, was the perfect opportunity to get rid of the "deadwood."

Today, he wasn't nearly as confident of the position he once embraced. Was improving the bottom line by terminating everyone over forty-five years old really the solution?

A well-stocked tackle box has the right combination of new and old.

■ ■ ■

An organization benefits by the right combination of new and old employees.

Frank had gone to a pay lake with Ellen several weeks ago. The owner promised they would catch fish. And they did. The fish—mostly brown and rainbow trout—were all young, hatchery-reared, and hit practically anything tossed into the water. The more Frank fished, the less enthusiastic he became. It was like shooting fish in a barrel.

Firms that downsize (or rightsize, reengineer, or reinvent themselves) simply as an excuse to reduce their overhead make a big mistake. When the dust settles, the remaining staff is too often composed of young, relatively inexperienced workers.

Fishy Business

Much like the hatchery trout in the pay lake Frank and Ellen fished.

While it is occasionally necessary to prune the deadwood—or redo the tackle box—it should be done with extreme care. If not, the reengineered company can end up with little institutional memory, no experienced mentors for younger workers, and little diversity in the ages of the employees. *Dumbsizing* is the term some give this thoughtless approach to downsizing.

At least partially due to these reasons, 70 percent or more of reengineered firms ultimately discover that they have merely replaced one set of problems with another. Sadly, these companies fail to recognize that a new, flashy red lure may not work as well as a battered (but still highly productive) old gray one.

CHAPTER 14

Take Me Back to
My Little Ice Shack

Although he had vowed not to go ice fishing that winter, Sunday afternoon found Frank trudging across Lake Lindner's frozen surface. After all, Mike had made it sound like a grand—albeit somewhat chilly—experience awaited him.

"You'll love it, sport," Mike said, pulling a portable ice shanty along behind him.

Frank looked off in the distance and spotted two or three groups of winter anglers already out on the ice. Some were in shanties similar to Mike's, and others were "hole hopping." With this procedure, the anglers drilled several openings and kept moving from one hole to another until they found a productive one.

The frigid wind brought tears coursing down Frank's cheeks; he wondered how long he could stand it. After the shanty was set up and a lantern turned on inside, he found the shelter almost toasty.

"Not bad, huh?" Mike asked.

Frank was not only surprised by the comfort of the shanty,

but by the productivity of the fishing. Using Mike's simple, stubby ice-fishing rods, both men caught plenty of sunfish.

"The fishing was even better last week," Mike said during a lull in the action.

"Were you catching mostly bluegills then?" Frank asked.

"Oh, no—I didn't come out at all last week. I got that report from Bob. The ice was too thin for me. I won't risk falling through no matter how good the fishing is."

No fish is worth dying for.

"Um, it's safe now, isn't it?" Frank asked a little hesitantly.

"Absolutely," Mike answered. "But you really have to be careful. There's a lot of ways you can get in trouble out here."

"Now you tell me," Frank said.

"Don't worry, when it comes to safety on the ice, I'm a dyed-in-the-wool sissy," Mike assured him. "Step out of the shanty and I'll show you something."

Mike pointed to a solitary fisherman several yards away. He told Frank that the man was probably catching lots of fish there, but it was risky.

"Why's that?"

"He's sitting right over a spring, and that means the ice there is a lot thinner than in most other spots on the lake," Mike explained.

"Why does he do it, then?"

"He usually catches plenty of fish, and so far he's been lucky," Mike said, shaking his head.

Mike rattled off other precautions concerning the frigid sport. He showed Frank a pair of wood-handled spikes he always carried in his coat pocket. "If you ever fall in, it can be almost impossible to get out," he explained. "Just jab these babies into the ice and you can drag yourself out hand over hand. In a pinch, a pocketknife or even car keys work pretty good."

Always leave yourself a way out.

Mike also carried a twenty-foot section of rope and a long chisel (called a "spud bar") that he poked the ice with to test its thickness. His last bit of advice was to always fish with a partner.

"Winter is one of the best times to catch fish, but you really should know what you're doing."

His mind at ease, Frank continued fishing. He was glad that Mike was blessed with good old-fashioned common sense.

I prefer my ice in a glass

Until Mike took him ice fishing, Frank's only experience with the sport came vicariously when he saw the movie *Grumpy Old Men*. And then he had paid more attention to Daryl Hannah

62

and Ann-Margret than to the ice-fishing scenes. Still, he was willing to give it a go. Good for him.

Being a comedy, *Grumpy Old Men* didn't set out to portray the dangerous side of ice fishing. But there's real peril in the sport, just as there is some degree of danger in fishing from a boat or even the bank. Mike seems to have his head on his shoulders; he's certainly not interested in taking unnecessary risks, no matter how good the fishing. The same lesson holds true in business. Every decision carries with it a degree of risk. Generally, the bigger the risk, the bigger the reward. But . . .

No fish is worth dying for.

■ ■ ■

Some deals should be left on the table.

Take the case of Lloyd's of London, one of the oldest and most respected names in the insurance underwriting business. Here's a company that should know something about risk and reward. So, how's Lloyd's doing nowadays? Not too well. Let's hope that by the time you read this, that pillar of British society has managed to set things right.

What in the world happened? Well, you could say that Lloyd's, in their haste to pull in big fish, may have taken their eyes off the ice. And it looks like the ice—in the form of a string of hurricanes, floods, oil spills, and some truly enormous claims from pollution and asbestos lawsuits—may have pulled them in instead.

Mike, on the other hand, was prepared for the worst. He wasn't about to risk his life for a fish or two. He carefully planned, not for the best outcome, but for the worst. He even carried a rope to help any unfortunate soul who broke through the ice. Must have been a Boy Scout.

Always leave yourself a way out.

■ ■ ■

Always leave others a way out.

Leaving a way out for yourself and others can be extremely important, in business as well as ice fishing. If you don't allow the other person a graceful way out—one that allows him or her to save face—you could end up with a real problem on your hands. This is true no matter how right you are, how many facts you have, or how logical your argument.

Some years ago an acquaintance decided that her most recent raise simply was not enough. She decided to confront her boss with the demand for a 20 percent raise. If she didn't get it, she'd walk. Surprisingly, he readily agreed not just to a 20 percent raise, but a 30 percent hike along with an impressive new title and long list of added responsibilities. All she had to do was relocate to Nuuk, Greenland.

We don't wish to insult our Greenland readers, but Nuuk (town motto: Bring Your Own Tent) is probably not on most vacationers' top-ten list. Our friend, who had acted without regard to the consequences, was shocked by the offer. When she recovered her composure somewhat, she hastily declined the offer and all the "perks" that went with it. Backing gracelessly out of the office, she considered herself lucky to have "gotten out of that one."

She made a big mistake in demanding a 20 percent raise, and nothing less. She left her boss with but two apparent alternatives: either give her the raise or let her walk. Her boss, however, was clever enough to find a response that let them both off the hook. She still wonders if he was bluffing.

CHAPTER 15

The Horror of Huggy Baits

Even though ice fishing had proved productive, it really wasn't Frank's cup of tea (make that iced tea). He found the sights, sounds, and especially the warmth of open-water fishing far superior to sitting motionless for hours over an enormous block of ice.

That didn't stop him from going out with Mike two more times that winter, but trundling over Lake Lindner's frozen surface in search of frostbitten fish just didn't do it for him. He did, however, enjoy the camaraderie of his fellow ice fishermen.

The winter anglers formed fairly tight groups on the ice and most were quite willing to share tips and tactics. No matter how invigorating the conversation, Frank usually headed toward the cozy confines of Mike's ice shanty before long.

When the weather warmed just enough to make the ice unsafe even for the most ardent ice fishermen, Frank stayed home dreaming of open-water fishing. He finally decided to take Mike's advice and use this time to get his gear in shape for spring.

His tackle boxes were messy, to say the least. In attempting to pick up a single shallow-diving crankbait, he found him-

65

self holding a tangled gob of lures, a phenomenon some refer to as "huggy baits."

Fortunately, Chuck had shown him a method of unraveling the mess by simply holding one of the lures in the cluster and shaking vigorously. Like magic, the baits dropped off one by one. After separation was completed, Frank set out to organize his tackle boxes, assigning each type of lure to a specific area.

Get the tackle box in shape *before* you go fishing.

Next, Frank sharpened every hook on every bait with a small file. He also got rid of lures and baits that hadn't won his confidence over the course of the season. The flashy red model Chuck had given him earlier was one of the discards. He finished up by cleaning and oiling his reels and spooling on fresh monofilament line.

It took a little longer than he'd thought, but Frank was pleased with the results. There was a time, not that long ago, when he would not have had the patience to bother with, much less accomplish, such a seemingly menial task. More surprising was the fact that he found it enjoyable as well as worthwhile. Now, when the weather finally broke, he would be ready.

An ounce of prevention . . .

Frank has obviously learned something about cleaning out a tackle box from his earlier experience with Chuck. He keeps what works, not necessarily what's new and shiny. We've talked about this "preparation thing" before, but it bears repeating. Many business problems could be avoided if some serious thought went into preparation. And preparation is, after all, just

one part of *prevention*. By preparing his tackle box and gear,
Frank prevents a lot of unnecessary problems.

**Get the tackle box in shape *before*
you go fishing.**

■ ■ ■

**Prevent problems now and you won't
have to solve them later.**

Let's examine this lesson from a different perspective—
that of medicine, which is certainly *big* business. Despite the
billions of dollars poured into research for cures for a plethora
of diseases, we are still plagued by these maladies. And new
afflictions like the Ebola virus, AIDS, and "mad cow" disease
seem to pop up with frightening regularity. To combat these
problems, still more money is pumped into the search for
cures and detection. This is important work, of course, but it
would make good sense to up the ante on *preventive* measures, too.

In 1996, U.K. Prime Minister John Majors reacted to the
spread of a serious health problem, bovine spongiform en-
cephalopathy ("mad cow" disease), not by calling for preventive measures, but by setting up a *war cabinet*. He even went
so far as to refer to the Germans, who were adamantly in favor
of a ban against British beef and dairy products, as the
"enemy." Like managers (and politicians) everywhere, he knew
that fighting wars can be more popular than finding real solu-
tions to real problems.

So, the war against disease continues. Proper diet and exercise, plus the removal of various ground, air, and water tox-
ins seems boring by comparison. And since it's doubtful that

anyone will ever win a Nobel Prize in medicine by advocating exercise, diet, and pollution reduction, the emphasis on prevention continues to lag.

Fishermen, on the other hand, know there are very real rewards for prevention. Boat, trailer, and motor maintenance—while not nearly as much fun as fishing—result in money saved and less inconvenience on the water. Maybe our health administrators and legislators need to go fishing a little more often.

CHAPTER 16

Look at That Baby Jump

"I haven't done this in a long, long time," O.A. said, scanning the bright blue water.

"It's like riding a bike; you never forget," Hank said, concentrating on what might have been a slight surface disturbance near a mangrove island. "Hey, we could just have some action over there."

O.A. looked in the direction of Hank's pointing finger and thought he saw a shadowy shape below the water's surface. His nine-foot fly rod sprang into action.

Hank watched admiringly as the white-haired angler made a picture-perfect cast that ended with his streamer setting down on the water with barely a ripple. As the brown lure slowly sank, O.A. pulled the line to make it mimic a darting baitfish. A large silvery mouth gulped it down.

In fishing, presentation means everything.

O.A. set the hook and the action began. He had almost forgotten just how hard tarpon could fight. Hank, shaking his head in amazement, watched his old friend expertly play the big fish. Although it had been years since he'd hooked a tarpon, O.A. hadn't lost a step.

When the moment all tarpon fishermen wait for finally took place, the powerful creature soared out of the water in a vertical jump that must have spanned nine feet. Even experienced fishermen sometimes freeze at the sight of such high-jumping acrobatics. O.A. didn't freeze. More than a half hour later, the tarpon finally tired and slowly turned on its side. O.A. lost no time in releasing the fish. It had been a grand fight.

"You still have it," Hank said, patting his friend on the back. "Bet you're glad you let me talk you into coming down to the Keys."

"Oh, I guess it beats watching April snowflakes," O.A. said, smiling.

"You're kidding?" Hank said, turning serious. "It doesn't really snow in April up there, does it?"

"Not very often," O.A. said.

"How in the world can you stand to live up north?"

"Good fishing," O.A. answered without hesitation.

"Does it really beat this?" Hank asked.

"It all depends," O.A. said. "At the end of a hard winter, you appreciate the fishing just that much more."

Hank laughed softly. "Man, you have one rosy outlook on life." What he thought, but didn't say, was that O.A.'s temperament was incredibly different now than in the days when he was younger, impulsive, and much more aggressive.

"So," O.A. said, changing the subject, "you're going to be doing a little work down here?"

"In Miami," Hank said. "Southern Systems is having some production problems."

"You're the guy who can set 'em straight," O.A. said with conviction.

"Well, I'll try," Hank said. "Say, do you see what I see?"

"This one's yours," O.A. said. As he watched Hank's

Fishy Business

streamer drop softly onto the water, he nodded in approval. He sure hoped it wouldn't be snowing when he got back home.

It's all in the delivery

Lucky O.A. He's basking in the sun while the guys and gals on Lake Lindner freeze their collective butts off. We find him with his old buddy Hank, who is still mightily impressed by the change between the O.A. he knew in his younger days and the calm and deliberate man fishing with him now. He's equally impressed by the way O.A. "delivers the bait."

 In fishing, presentation means everything.

■ ■ ■

In business, presentation is essential.

Like it or not, a good manager needs to develop the right touch in delivering his or her story. We've seen many bright, dedicated, and earnest young people fail—sometimes miserably—because of a poor presentation.

Frank Gilbreth is a name known to most managers and industrial engineers. One of the founders of Scientific Management, he had a wealth of ideas—many of which are currently being touted as new and original concepts to an audience with little knowledge or interest in anything that happened before 1996.

Frank and wife, Lillian were equal partners in these efforts, and their life story was captured in the book and film, *Cheaper by the Dozen*. But Frank Gilbreth got off to a rocky start.

Despite an abundance of brilliant ideas, he made little impact early on in his career. A wise friend made an observation Gilbreth never forgot. *An idea is just an idea until it is written down.* His 1911 book, *Motion Study,* effectively served to outline and promote his belief in this "one best way." He followed up with additional books that further documented his ideas, and served as blueprints for others.

Today's manager still needs to present his or her ideas on paper, of course; but it has become even more important to do so orally. Some managers rely on the razzle-dazzle of computer-generated presentations. We're not about to say that these trimmings don't play a role in audience acceptance. But ultimately, real thought and a solid plan must be behind the glitz.

O.A. could have made a "colorful" or noisy cast, but it wouldn't have had the same effect on the object of his interest, the tarpon. Similarly, in business, a properly organized presentation—*with substance*—plays a vital role in getting your ideas across.

CHAPTER 17

Ouch!

Winter had passed all too slowly for Frank. Now, waiting impatiently for milder weather, he whiled away his leisure time reading angling books and watching a host of fishing experts on TV. He was, in fact, watching one of his favorites, Long John Short, when the phone rang. He hesitated a moment for fear that it might be Big Jake, intent on continuing the argument that they had at work that day. If nothing else, the man was relentless. Sighing, he picked the phone up.

"Hi, Frank—it's O.A.," the voice announced.

"O.A.?" Frank said, surprised by the call. Even though the ace fisherman had never been anything but congenial, Frank was always a little nervous around him.

"Yep, in the flesh . . . or over the phone, I should say."

"I thought you were in Florida."

"Got back Tuesday," O.A. said. His tarpon trip had merely whetted his appetite to get out on the water again. "Well, are you ready to do some fishing?"

"Always," Frank said. "As soon as it warms up a little, I'll be on Lake Lindner. You can bet on it."

"It's warm enough right now, partner," O.A. said. "I'm heading out to Circle Creek tomorrow. Interested?"

"Sure," Frank said, excited at the prospect of finally getting to fish with the local legend, "but what's hitting this early in the year?"

"A number of species, actually, but I'm interested in pike. They should be active about now."

Successful fishermen have a plan.

"Count me in," Frank said. O.A. gave directions to the launch site and told Frank to bring along a hefty rod outfitted with stout line. Frank thought that he would at least be prepared for the chilly conditions after the time he had spent ice fishing.

When Frank arrived at the creek the next morning, O.A. already had the boat in the water. "Let's get those northerns," O.A. said, and the two fishermen shoved off.

"Just remember, these guys have sharp choppers. I don't mean to insult you, but don't try to land them like you would a bass. Stick your hand in a pike's mouth and we just might be making an unexpected trip to the emergency room."

O.A. explained that although live minnows might deliver more pike, he planned to cast shallow-diving crankbaits to the "snakes." "Sometimes they'll bite right through the line, but not as often as you might think."

Before they reached a wood-filled spot near a beaver lodge, O.A. carefully set out everything they would need to do the job.

Fishy Business

As was his custom, the net was given a special place of honor where it could be grabbed quickly by either man. Pliers were laid out within easy reach and the tackle boxes were closed tight.

"A guy I knew brought in a big pike a couple of years back," O.A. said. "The fish came in pretty easily and he lifted it into the boat. Well, that sort of woke the pike up and it managed to squirm loose. The guy had two tackle boxes open and the pike thrashed and jumped all over the boat. Lures were flying everywhere. He ended up with a pretty nice pike, but also with a hook in his hand."

Noticing the look on Frank's face, O.A. assured him that they would experience nothing of that sort. "You never know what's going to happen with a pike, but we're prepared about as well as we can be," he said. "Now, let's get a big, toothy water wolf! What do you say?"

Anticipate the positive, eliminate the negative . . . .

Frank is clearly delighted to have an opportunity to fish with a local legend. He realizes that the fastest way to become a better fisherman is to fish with the experts. Ronnie and Mike have taught him a great deal; the Old Angler is likely to teach him much more.

One of the lessons that Frank should take away from this particular excursion is the importance of being proactive—of anticipating just what might happen and preparing for that eventuality. O.A. explained to Frank that based on the time of year and prevailing conditions, northern pike should be active and hungry about now. This way of thinking is in total contrast to the angler who depends on luck and fishes for "whatever will take the bait."

Successful fishermen have a plan.

■ ■ ■

Good managers are proactive, not reactive.

James P. Ignizio and Bill Ignizio

The story O.A. told about the angler who didn't anticipate the consequences of landing an angry pike in a small boat is an example of the misfortunes that can befall those who don't plan ahead. And, of course, once the fish was in the hapless fisherman's boat, about all he could do was react.

Many managers routinely react to situations rather than anticipate them. Frank himself has been guilty of this more than a time or two. With this energy-draining philosophy, a great deal of time is spent worrying about losing instead of planning to succeed.

One notable example would be our country's reaction to the news, in 1957, of the launch of Sputnik. The fact that the Russians had placed a satellite in orbit, and done so before us, was shattering. We hadn't even anticipated that possibility. So we *reacted*. The president set, as the nation's goal, the landing of our astronauts on the moon—before the Russians, of course.

We thought we were in a race when in fact we were running solo. We landed our astronauts on the moon in 1969, and won the contest. But it was a hollow victory since the Russians never even made it to the arena, much less out of the starting blocks.

CHAPTER 18

A Tale of Toothy Terrors

The spot O.A. had chosen to fish looked good to Frank. Besides the mound of branches and limbs that made up the beaver lodge, there were a number of fallen trees extending from the bank into the water. In short, it appeared to be a particularly fishy place.

"Just work your lure slowly," O.A. advised. "Even though pike like cool water, they probably won't be moving too fast this early in the year. I'd reel in the bait without any fancy moves."

"You don't give 'em the old zigzag retrieve?" Frank asked, referring to a tactic he sometimes used to catch bass.

"You could, I suppose, but I like to bring the lure right back to the boat. Pike are built for speed, not cornering," O.A. explained.

Don't fish for pike like you would bass.

Frank, who was prepared for a long day on the water, cast out his plug. An elongated shape appeared from nowhere and smacked it. The jolt was like an electric current running through the line to the rod handle.

The thrashing pike shot skyward, shaking its head in an attempt to lose the lure. Frank sat in fascination, watching the sleek creature as it dropped back to the water, producing a spray that doused him. He almost felt like someone else had hooked the fish. Then it was over, and the fish was gone. It was not so much that he had reacted slowly; it was more like he had hardly reacted at all.

"Fun while it lasted, wasn't it?" O.A. said, chuckling.

"I really messed up," Frank moaned. How could he sit there zombielike as the pike flipped and flopped all over the place?

"Don't be so hard on yourself. That was your first pike, after all. I'm willing to bet you won't make that mistake again."

O.A. certainly didn't make any mistakes with the fish he hooked a few minutes later. He held the rod high and quickly reeled in a small but spirited northern pike. Frank managed to handle the net efficiently if not expertly.

"Good netting job, partner," O.A. said, using pliers to unhook the lure from the pike's toothy jaws.

By the time O.A. had landed his third pike, a nice sevenpounder, Frank realized why everyone at Bob's Bait and Tackle held the man in such high esteem. He fished almost flawlessly with seemingly little effort.

It was nearly time to head back to the ramp when Frank hooked a northern of his own. This time, he followed O.A.'s advice to the letter, keeping the rod pointing skyward to draw the fish away from cover. O.A. waited silently, net in hand.

The fish suddenly regained its strength, dragging line off the reel. Frank kept the rod tip high and cranked when the pike finally stopped pulling. He maintained his cool when the unseen quarry unexpectedly dived beneath the boat, and slowly regained the upper hand, steadily bringing the fish boatward.

"Got him!" O.A. said, scooping up the pike. And it was over just that soon, with the biggest fish Frank had ever caught safely in the net.

Fishy Business

"Great job!" O.A. said. "And a great fish, too!"

Frank surprised himself by having O.A. set the fish free. It had fought well, and who knows—maybe he'd catch it again another day.

We're all the same, just different

Frank has just discovered that you might have to use a radically different style of fishing depending on the type of fish you are after. Try fishing for pike like you would a bass and you will probably be disappointed. Try landing a pike like a bass and you'll learn a lesson you won't soon forget.

 Don't fish for pike like you would bass.

■ ■ ■

Know your customer.

This same lesson holds just as true in business on a global scale. Don't expect your Japanese client, or customer, to act like your Brazilian client, or customer. This has nothing to do with stereotypes. People of different cultures and religions simply react in different ways to precisely the same situation. By wearing leather shoes and accessories, for instance, you could offend your Hindu clients, who revere cows. TV and the worldwide spread of familiar franchise restaurants is reducing, to some degree, these differences. Perhaps sometime in the future we will all act the same, think the same, and look the same—and wouldn't that be boring. Until then, we need to appreciate that there are differences and become, as advised in the previous chapter, proactive rather than reactive.

One little *faux pas* that occurred as a consequence of ignoring cultural differences was the introduction of the VW Rabbit in the United States. For some reason, VW management thought that "rabbit" was a name that would inspire Americans to buy Volkswagens. After all, we had gobbled up VW "beetles" by the hundreds of thousands.

Whatever the case, Americans seem to have difficulty imagining themselves driving rabbits. Mustangs maybe, but certainly not rabbits. American managers have made similar mistakes. Like trying to sell cars with left-side steering wheels to customers in countries where they drive on the left.

CHAPTER 19

Star Pupil

Frank's triumphant pike outing was marred only by the fact that he was unable to fish with O.A. again for the next several weeks. Big Jake's angry and misdirected attempts to solve the mounting problems at work took up more and more of Frank's time. Worst of all, Jake's demands that he check out each and every idea and notion were becoming increasingly desperate. While none of this helped, it certainly diminished Frank's time spent on the water.

Ellen, in the meantime, had begun watching some of Frank's favorite fishing shows partly out of curiosity and partly to kibitz. It didn't take long before she found herself caught up in the action.

"That was a huge pike," she said after one program. "Was the one you caught that big?"

"About half that size," Frank admitted.

"Do you think O.A. would mind if I tagged along with you boys sometime?"

Frank was caught by surprise. Although she had been a good sport about his new hobby, he didn't think that she was particularly excited about it.

"Hey, what can I say? I guess all of these TV shows and this constant chatter about fishing have me brainwashed," Ellen said. "I'm ready to get out there and catch some hawgs!"

"Hawgs?"

"Isn't that what the bass guys call them?"

"That's what they call them," Frank said, smiling and shaking his head.

Later that evening Frank called O.A. and learned that he was free to fish the following weekend. Unfortunately, Frank was once again tied up.

"Well, it looks like O.A. and I can't connect—not for a while, at least," he told Ellen after hanging up.

"Darn, I really wanted to fish with the great man," Ellen said dejectedly.

"You will. I told him *you* could make it, and he said he'd meet you at the lake this Saturday." Ellen was flustered, and protested that she would embarrass herself.

"Hey, I fished with him and I'm not exactly a pro," Frank said. "Besides, he's a great guy. And, believe me, you won't embarrass yourself. You cast better than I do, for Pete's sake."

Ellen finally gave in, but not without misgivings. She was still a little apprehensive when she arrived at the lake the following Saturday. O.A. sensed it and quickly set her mind at ease.

"Ellen, just think of me as your guide. It's my job to find the fish, and yours to relax and have fun."

Ellen marveled at O.A.'s boat-handling ability and skill with a fishing rod. Not only that, he seemed to be acutely tuned in to everything around him—the birds, the trees, and even the breeze.

As the wind whipped up a little, O.A. told Ellen of a poem he had learned long ago:

> "Wind from the north,
> Fishermen don't go forth.
> Wind from the south,
> Fish take bait in the mouth.
> Wind from the east,
> Fish hit the least.

Fishy Business

Wind from the west,
Fish hit the best."

"Is that poem reliable?" Ellen asked.

"Sometimes," O.A. said, "but it's *always* great for excuses when you don't catch fish."

As they fished near a small island, Ellen noticed a silvery glint out of the corner of her eye, then a second and a third. She set down her rod and watched. From time to time, a small fish would skip and skitter over the water's surface. She pointed this out to O.A.

"Good eyes. Those little fish aren't dancing for joy, you can bet," O.A. said. "They're trying to get away from what's chasing them."

"What do you think's after them?"

"I suspect it's bass. Let's go get 'em, partner."

O.A. suggested that Ellen tie on a crankbait that ran only a foot or two deep when retrieved. She tossed it out, but nothing happened. O.A., in the meantime, quickly hauled in two lively bass. When Ellen asked  what she was doing wrong, he showed her how slowly he was working the lure.

"Crank the reel handle at the same speed I do," he said. "That's right. Keep the lure coming in real slow."

Encourage the novice.

After the mini-lesson, Ellen was ready to try again. A two-pound largemouth smacked the plug, putting on a fine display of head-shaking gyrations. Although the action began to tail off within several minutes, she managed to catch another bass while O.A. caught two more. The highlight of the day for Ellen, however, came when the Old Angler told her she was one of the best beginners he had ever seen. She was hooked.

Mentoring—it's time to give a little

O.A. has served as a mentor for both Frank and Ellen, and many others before them. The good mentor gets as much satisfaction out of the success of his or her student as does the student. Few things in life are more satisfying than to pass on your knowledge to someone who appreciates—and uses—it. And all of us want to be told we are doing well. A few words of encouragement from a mentor can work wonders—for both parties.

 Encourage the novice.

■ ■ ■

There's more to management than giving orders.

Unfortunately, many workers are called into the manager's office only when they have either done something to displease the boss, or are ordered to take on some new task. The way some bosses grudgingly dole out words of encouragement and praise, you would think they must be terribly expensive. If that was the case, Big Jake would have a personal savings account that would be the envy of Silas Marner.

A manager we know is notorious for rarely having a good word for his employees. If you are asked to Mr. X's office, chances are it's going to be unpleasant. When this was pointed out to him, he paused for a moment and said: "I'm not here to win any popularity contest; I'm just here to win." Case closed. Mind shut.

Thankfully, not all managers emulate Mr. X. Ms. Y, for example, can be firm—but without rancor. Unlike Mr. X, she doesn't demand blind obedience. Instead, she willingly discusses the issues, seeks her subordinate's opinions, and looks for a mutually acceptable course of action.

Most important, Ms. Y takes time to thank a subordinate for work well done, and to praise him or her for a particularly outstanding job. She is convinced that this "extra effort" is a sound investment—in her future, her employees' futures, and the future of the company itself.

When was the last time you thanked one of your workers? Encouraged a new hire? And when was the last time the boss thanked *you*?

CHAPTER 20

If You Believe That . . .

Frank was overjoyed that Ellen's outing with O.A. had been successful. She told him of O.A.'s simple tip to slow down the retrieval speed of her lure. As far as Ellen was concerned, the man was a genius. Frank agreed.

He was especially happy when he and O.A. were able to connect that weekend and go fishing on Lake Lindner. He was shocked, however, when by day's end he had caught two bass to O.A.'s one. O.A. seemed genuinely happy for Frank, and told the boys at Bob's Bait and Tackle that Frank would most likely be turning pro soon.

"This young man fishes almost as well as his wife!" O.A. proclaimed, patting Frank on the back.

"Well, Frank," Mike said, "I think it's time I took you fishing for bugle-mouth bass."

"Bugle-mouth bass?" Frank said, narrowing his eyes suspiciously.

Don't believe *everything* you hear on
the water.

"Yep, we catch 'em at Circle Creek. And it's not unusual to get a ten- or twelve-pounder there," Mike said. That perked Frank up.

After Mike and Frank had set up the trip, O.A. took Frank aside and explained that medium-to-heavy tackle would be best. He also advised him to take along a supply of sinkers and a five-gallon bucket similar to those used by some of the ice fishermen Frank had observed over the winter.

"You've never mentioned bugle-mouth bass," Frank told O.A.

"It will be an experience," O.A. said, walking out the door. Ronnie could be heard chuckling in the background.

When Frank told Ellen of his upcoming bugle-mouth bass trip with Mike, she gave him a quizzical look. "You think he was putting you on? Maybe it's some type of initiation into the gang." Frank would just have to wait to find out.

The day of the Great Bugle-mouth Bash was dreary. Icy raindrops spit from dark gray clouds in the early hours of the morning. When Frank arrived at the designated spot, Mike was already there, with his rod perched on a forked stick and sitting on a five-gallon bucket. Frank sat down next to him on his own bucket.

"Make yourself at home," Mike said, not looking in Frank's direction. His eyes were focused on his fishing rod.

"We're going to fish from shore?" Frank asked.

"Best way in the world to catch bugle-mouths," Mike assured him. "Now bait up, big guy." He handed Frank an opened can of corn.

"Trout?" Frank asked, taking the corn from Mike's hand.

"What's that?" Mike asked.

"I've heard trout like corn. Is that what we're *really* fishing for?"

"Nope, not much in the way of trout in these waters," Mike said. "Now bait up, bud."

"You think this hook will be okay?" Frank asked.

Sparing just a second or two to look, Mike told him to try a smaller hook. Bugle-mouth bass, he informed Frank, sometimes require a delicate presentation.

"There it is," Mike said, interrupting his own discussion of hook sizes. He was staring at his rod.

"There's what?" Frank asked.

"Look at my line. See it twitch?"

Frank didn't see anything, but he intently stared at the line. Then he noticed an almost imperceptible movement. Something in the creek was nibbling at Mike's bait.

Mike picked up the rod, cranked in slack line, and set the hook. The fight was on. The rod bowed and line played off the reel. The unseen fish made its way into the stream current and pulled yet more line off the reel. Mike began to slowly gain on the fish. Frank was astounded by the creature's strength.

Mike finally cranked the battling bugle-mouth in toward shore. Frank picked up the net, but the fish wasn't finished yet. The surge wasn't quite as strong as before, though, and Mike once again brought his uncooperative quarry back.

At last, Frank could see the shape of the fish under the water's roiling surface. It was a carp, and a big one. As he attempted to net it, the fish jerked away at the last instant. Frank succeeded only in bumping the net against the side of the bruiser.

"Got him," he said at last. "He's a big one."

Mike estimated the carp's weight at about ten pounds. And, yes, this beauty was the fabled Circle Creek "bugle-mouth bass."

One's man's trash fish is another man's treasure.

Fishy Business

"Ronnie told me you had never fished for carp before," Mike said, prying the hook free from the fish's mouth.

"So, he was in on it, too?"

"Of course, and so was O.A., and Bob and—"

"I get the picture," Frank said. "Have a little fun with the new guy."

"Not mad, are you?"

"Yes! Mad that *I* haven't caught one yet. Do they always hit this light?"

Sometimes, Mike explained, carp dispense with the delicate touch this particular fish had displayed and simply yank the rod into the water. They could also be wary, and this seemed to be one of those days.

Frank quickly stabbed several kernels of corn on his hook and tossed out the bait. He was ready to catch a bugle-mouth bass of his own.

Watch out for the punch line

When Frank heard about Circle Creek's fabled bugle-mouth bass, he suspected that the bait-shop boys were pulling a joke on him. He didn't mind; it was harmless good fun. Sometimes, though, what you hear can be damaging—at least, if you accept it without reservation. In business, care must be taken so as not to be drawn into wild speculation or irresponsible action based on hearsay or idle gossip.

 You can't believe everything you hear on the water.

■ ■ ■

You can't believe everything you hear around the water cooler.

James P. Ignizio and Bill Ignizio

Frank enjoyed Mike's tale of the "bugle-mouth bass" as much as the regulars at Bob's. The carp outing also added to Frank's ever-growing cache of angling knowledge. Just a few of the many things he learned that day included these gems:

Fishing from shore can be as much fun as fishing in a boat.

Fish only nibble if the hook is too big.

Fishing is supposed to be fun.

Carp, considered a "trash fish" by some, are really an underrated fish.

 One man's trash fish is another man's treasure.

■ ■ ■

The most menial task can have value.

In fishing, as in business, you'll learn a lot more if you keep alert. Consider one young college graduate's experience. As a "rookie," he was assigned to do jobs that the veterans weren't interested in, like keeping track of bathroom and copy-machine inventory. Admonished to never let the toilet-paper supply get low, our hero—let's call him Jack—decided to automate this routine chore.

Using a personal computer and some software (mainly a spreadsheet package), he devoted considerable time and energy to putting together a computerized program for monitoring inventory. Seemed like a pretty ho-hum task.

The package allowed him to take care of the toilet-paper problem without spending much time. This, in turn, enabled Jack to get involved in other projects. But, he wondered, could there be a market for his inventory package? Maybe not in

90

Fishy Business

monitoring toilet-paper reserves, but in, say, shoes or clothing sales.

Without much effort, Jack quickly found an eager market for his product. He started by selling to small businesses, and did the installation, checkout, and maintenance himself. When he found himself with more business than he could handle alone, he quit his job (they're back to taking care of the toilet-paper inventory manually) and hired a few people to help. Today he has a thriving business.

There are some people, however, who are above such "menial" tasks. They prefer not to get their hands dirty, even if it leads to an increased understanding of the company. In the nation of Mali, these kinds of managers are easy to spot.

To show others that they are not farmers, factory workers, or anything that commonplace or unimportant, the fingernail of the little finger on the right hand is grown to extreme length. While crops rot in the field or machines stand idle, the long fingernails keep shuffling paper. And Mali, with a per capita income of less than three hundred dollars, remains one of the poorest nations on earth. They could learn a lot from Jack.

CHAPTER 21

Say Cheese . . . or Carp

Frank stared so intently at his fishing line, he thought he might end up with one whopper of a headache. He was still looking for any suspicious twitch, twitter, or vibration when a gray-haired angler set up camp several yards downstream.

After Mike caught his fish, the action ground to a halt. But he assured Frank that this was the way of "bugle-mouth bass." They could ignore the bait for hours and then suddenly begin feeding with wild abandon. Frank's patience paid off when a carp gobbled up his corn-encrusted hook and ran downstream.

"Thank you, Jolly Green Giant," Frank shouted, grabbing his rod and holding on tight. The fish stripped off line so quickly he thought it might empty his reel.

Remembering O.A.'s words, Frank kept the rod tip high and cranked the reel handle whenever the fish stopped its run. Grudgingly, the carp came in. Mike scooped up the copper-colored bottom feeder with one deft jab of the net and handed it to Frank. Frank unhooked the oversized minnow and eased it back into Circle Creek.

"Hey, I should have snapped your picture," Mike said, smacking his forehead. "Well, you'll catch a bigger one, and I'll get that baby on film."

Mike's prophecy came to pass. Just a few minutes later, Frank was straining to land a second carp, much larger than the first. Out of the corner of his eye, he noticed Mike running toward his own rod. They both had fish on at the same time!

"Lift your rod up so I can cross under it," Mike shouted.

Frank obliged and Mike stepped under the raised rod, following his errant carp. After a minute or so, Mike managed to land his fish. Frank's fish wasn't finished yet.

"You're doing good," Mike said, watching the struggle. "Man, that's gotta be a nice fish."

It was only a matter of minutes, though it seemed like hours to Frank, until Mike finally netted the carp. Frank never imagined a fish could fight that hard. This time Mike remembered the camera, and snapped several photos of Frank proudly displaying his trophy—a fifteen-pound bugle-mouth. Neither man noticed their downstream neighbor approaching.

Walking past them, the gray-haired angler, who had also been fishing for carp, stomped by. Frank thought he heard him mumble something about some guys having "all the luck."

"Not luck, Edgar. It's skill, carp-fishing skill," Mike called out to the man.

Edgar's response was brief but clear: "Idiot."

When the man was out of earshot, Frank asked: "What was that all about?"

"Nothing really," Mike said. "That's just poor ol' sour Edgar. He hates when he doesn't catch fish, and he hates it even more when someone else does. It's kind of sad, actually."

 If fishing isn't fun, you're doing something wrong.

Mike explained that while Edgar had been fishing for a long time, he hadn't improved much over the years. He felt that fishing success was mainly due to luck, and that if he fished long enough, his luck was bound to change. Not too surprisingly, it never did.

Care to have a little whine with that?

There's an exception to every rule, and ol' Edgar is ours. Fishing has helped Frank to relax and look at the bigger picture while viewing life as an experience to be relished. But it sure hasn't changed Edgar, who sees everything as a bitter struggle. Worse yet, he blames everyone but himself for his problems. He's in a war, and losing.

You may have an Edgar of your own at work. He's the kind of guy that you dread seeing at the doorway to your office or cubicle. He is the Bearer of Bad Tidings, the Crown Prince of Doom and Gloom, and the King of Carping (pun intended). And my, can he whine.

Folks such as Edgar find it hard to change. After years of perfecting these skills, whining and complaining have become second nature to them. When dealing with this type, keep in mind that whiners can damage the morale of everyone around them, including you.

If fishing isn't fun, you're doing something wrong.

■ ■ ■

If you can't cure the whine, replace the whiner.

Fishy Business

Think about it this way: Imagine being stuck out on the middle of a lake, in a small boat, with someone like ol' Edgar. Not a pretty picture, is it? It's small wonder that a lot of folks simply refuse to fish with him. We feel their pain.

But how do you deal with a whiner in a real-life situation? Reactions we've observed too often range from brutal to futile.

Some managers "declare war" on the whiner, making things so uncomfortable for him that he surrenders—and leaves. With this course of action, you risk the possibility of transforming your offender into a martyr, the victim of yet another heartless boss. Worse yet, even if this tactic works, *you* lose a little of your own humanity.

Henry Ford is said to have dealt with managers he intended to fire in a less-than-sensitive manner. He allegedly moved every bit of furniture out of their offices—and sometimes even had it chopped into neatly stacked kindling. It seems unlikely that this practice made him any richer or happier. It most certainly didn't help the victims of his wrath or improve the morale of the company.

Then, of course, there is the "kinder, gentler" approach. With this method, you talk to the whiner, reason with him and see if he can be convinced to change his ways. Sometimes this works. Other times, though, it's like asking a giraffe to keep his head down.

If your whiner won't change no matter what you do, termination may be your only option. Fortunately, there is often hope—even for someone like sour ol' Edgar. Sometimes not. We'll see.

CHAPTER 22

Poster Boy

Although Frank didn't go out of his way to tell anyone, he had truly enjoyed fishing for carp with Mike. He liked it so much, in fact, that he had fished Circle Creek for "bugle-mouths" twice the previous week after work. But now it was time to get in a little bassin' with Ronnie.

As he walked through the door of Bob's Bait and Tackle, Frank was confronted by a poster-size picture of him and his whopper carp. The blowup, taped to the wall, was impossible to miss. Mike had been a busy boy.

Bob, pretending to tidy up the counter, greeted Frank with a casual wave. "Nice photo, huh?" he said a little too sincerely.

"Hey, you saw your pitcher." Ronnie had burst on the scene.

"I'm sure I'm not the only one who's seen it," Frank said.

"That'd be a good bet. Well, we gonna stand 'round yappin' 'bout your carp or are we goin' bassin'?"

"Bassing, please," Frank said.

"You boys have a good time, now," Bob instructed as they turned to leave. "And don't worry, Frank—I'll take good care of your photo for you."

Fishy Business

"You're a peach," Frank called out.

Ronnie lost no time in heading the boat toward a weedy bay. "You're gonna be in bass heaven," he promised.

Shutting off the outboard several yards from the bay, Ronnie used the electric trolling motor to quietly work his way in. He showed Frank the simple setup they would be fishing: an unweighted "motor oil" plastic worm rigged "Texas style."

Frank rigged up and they began. Ronnie was quickly into the first bass of the day . . . and the second, and the third. Frank had learned the importance of taking the time to observe, and that's just what he did. But he still couldn't figure out Ronnie's secret.

"Want a tip, Frank?" Ronnie asked, replacing a tattered worm with a fresh one.

"Absolutely."

"Watch your line. I know you're probably used to *feelin'* bass hit, but these fish is nibblin' real light. So, if you see that line move at all, just rear back on your rod."

The best tip is one you understand.

Ronnie's advice seemed simple enough, and best of all, it worked. In a matter of moments, Frank was into his first bass of the day. He found the method surprisingly similar to the carp-fishing technique he and Mike had used at Circle Creek. That day, too, they had concentrated on line movement rather than feeling the strike. He simply hadn't considered using the tactic for bass.

When Frank got the hang of it, he began to match Ronnie bass for bass. After the feeding frenzy ended, the tally for the two anglers was a dozen bass taken in a little over an hour's time. Frank was delighted—not simply due to the fish he'd caught, but because he was finally developing the patience and understanding it took to catch them *consistently.*

"Frank, you're turnin' into a fine fisherman," Ronnie said on the way back to the ramp.

"I've been lucky," Frank said. "I've had some good teachers."

What we have here is a failure to communicate

One of the most important attributes of a good manager is the ability and willingness to communicate. Ronnie's advice to Frank was clear, concise, and immediately useful. Like another Ronnie before him, he is a "great communicator."

 The best tip is one you understand.

■ ■ ■

Communicate clearly and concisely.

Interestingly, some people you might think would be terrific communicators are not. Years of schooling seem to encourage the use of specialized jargon at the expense of plain old English. MBAs, engineers, and scientists are three groups that are especially prone to this pitfall. They rely on terminology that may be comprehensible to them, but is gibberish to the rest of the world.

While Frank's immediate superior's writing skills are adequate, his use of the spoken word leaves something to be desired—although it's hardly a consequence of an overly complex vocabulary. Just last week, Big Jake burst into Frank's office and shouted: "I want you to kick some butt. Make sure those goons in Building C don't screw up again. And tell that jerk Bates that if things don't change fast he'd better start looking for another job."

A shaken Frank only had time to nod once in the affirmative before Jake slammed the door shut as he stormed out. Frank didn't know what to make of it all. Hadn't Jake read his

Fishy Business

reports concerning the problems in Building C? They clearly showed that Ed Bates was hardly a jerk.

In fact, Frank had slowly and grudgingly come to appreciate Bates's thoughtful, low-key approach to problem solving. The man was not flashy, just competent. Jake, of course, considered the fifty-something Bates an "over-the-hill wimp." Frank thought he couldn't have been more wrong. He was becoming convinced that the problems at the plant shouldn't be placed on the shoulders of people like Bates.

But Frank resisted the temptation to rush over to Jake's office. He had learned the hard way that his boss didn't have the time or patience for explanations. As Jake had told another subordinate, "This is a war, son. If you don't follow my orders the first time, there ain't gonna be a second chance."

Frank believed him.

CHAPTER 23

Frank Meets the Trollers

Having caught a dozen bass, Frank and Ronnie were content to call it a morning. As Ronnie meandered back to the ramp, he noticed a familiar boat trolling parallel to the opposite shoreline. He headed over in that direction.

"There's a couple a guys I want you to meet," he shouted above the outboard's roar. Getting the attention of the two fishermen, Ronnie waved them over.

"Ronnie, how you doing?" the man in the bow asked.

"Dandy, you fellas catchin' anything?"

"Eight bass, I think," the bow rider, Mark, calculated. "Is that right, Art?" Art nodded.

After making introductions all the way around, Ronnie asked Mark to show Frank what they had been catching their bass on. The lure was unlike anything Frank had ever seen before.

"What do you call it?" he asked.

"That's a Troll Tiger," Mark said, handing Frank what appeared to be a misshapen metal plug, with hooks dangling off it. "We just drag it around the lake hoping something will take a swipe at it."

100

Fishy Business

"Kinda looks like a cow stomped on, don't it, Frank?" Ronnie said, handing the lure back to Mark.

Frank had to agree that Ronnie's description was pretty accurate. After the trollers had returned to their trolling, Frank asked Ronnie about the strange lures the men used.

"They work, you can bet on it," Ronnie said. "But as far as them draggin' the things 'round the lake, there's a little more to it than that."

"I figured as much."

"You figured right. Them guys have dozens a plugs like that in sizes that run at different depths," Ronnie explained. "They also troll the same kind of crankbaits we do."

"So they basically fish pretty much like we do," Frank said.

"There's more to it than that, ol' buddy. Them fellas have trollin' down to a fine science. And they hardly ever get skunked," Ronnie said.

"Is the Troll Tiger the reason?" Frank asked.

"It don't hurt none. But the important thing is what they know, not what they fish," Ronnie said.

"And just what *do* they know?" Frank asked.

Know the lay of the lake.

"Where every little nook and cranny on this lake happens to be. There ain't a channel, point, bar, breakline, or bump on ol' Lake Lindner them two don't know 'bout. And that, Frank, ol' buddy, is why they catch lots a fish."

Hey, those are new shoes!

Not many people knew that Frank's fiery boss Big Jake left his previous job after he had been there for only a few months. It wasn't because he didn't like it. Along with a fat paycheck, there was plenty of mahogany, leather chairs, a wet bar, and one hellacious view of the city. What was not to like?

Know the lay of the lake.

■ ■ ■

Know the lay of the land.

Everything went swimmingly until Margaret, a member of Jake's staff, informed him of a serious problem. His first executive decision had been to order production to proceed, as he never tired of bellowing, "full steam ahead." Yet they were currently producing so many pressboard computer workstations that they had run out of places to store them.

Jake wasn't worried about that, just annoyed. He demanded that room be found to accommodate the overflowing inventory—or that Vince (or was it Victor?) in marketing do something to increase sales. Margaret didn't seem to appreciate this logic.

"Sir," she said, "why not take a look for yourself? I think you'll see that there's no floor space to spare. Before you blame marketing, why not check out the product demand estimates I put in your in-box three weeks ago?"

"Young woman," Jake replied icily, "this is a two-thousand-dollar suit and those are brand-new six-hundred-dollar shoes."

"I'm not sure I understand," Margaret said . . . understandably.

"There ain't no way," Jake continued in his most condescending manner, "that I'm going to wade through all that dust down there in the trenches just to check out the accommodations. And if what's-his-name in marketing has anything to tell me, he knows where my office is."

Fishy Business

Jake was looking for a new job the next day. Margaret, it turned out, was the niece of the company CEO. And the marketing director (whose name was Vance, not Vince or Victor) married Margaret less than a month after Jake got the sack. He was *not* invited to the wedding.

Talk about learning the lay of the land the hard way.

CHAPTER 24

Great Day at Lake Lindner

Frank's introduction to the trollers was another revelation in his meandering quest to become the Compleat Angler. Here was yet another productive method he had never tried. How many more were there?

Ronnie's advice was simple. "Be patient and just stick with what you know for now."

The two men looked up as O.A. and Chuck walked through the door of the bait shop. O.A. walked over to join them while Chuck stopped to speak with Bob.

"How'd you guys do out there today?" O.A. asked.

"Pitiful," Ronnie said. "Ol' Frank and me was just moanin' about how little we know about bass fishin'."

Fishy Business

"That's too bad," O.A. commiserated. "Did you catch a few, at least?"

"Oh, just a dozen or so," Ronnie said, straight-faced.

O.A. gave him a playful swipe with his fishing hat. "And you had me feeling sorry for you," he said, shaking his head in mock anger.

"How'd you and Chuck do today?" Ronnie asked.

"A couple." It was O.A.'s typical response. Ronnie looked back at Chuck, who had overheard the question. He held up nine fingers to indicate how many bass they had caught.

"Say, we ran into Mark and Art while we was out," Ronnie said.

"I'm sure they caught their share," O.A. said.

"They caught them trolling," Frank said.

O.A. wasn't surprised. "Sounds like Mark and Art."

"I was just telling Ronnie that there's just so many ways to catch fish that it's . . . well, it's . . ."

"Kind of mind-boggling," O.A. finished Frank's sentence for him.

O.A. assured Frank that there were, indeed, numerous ways to catch the many species that inhabited Lake Lindner, and all of the other waters they fished. He agreed with Ronnie that you just had to relax and learn as you went along.

"But how do you know which way is best?" Frank asked. "Or is that a stupid question?"

"Absolutely not," O.A. said. "Frank, I don't want to hedge, but it all depends."

"Boy, I'd hate to hear you hedge." Ronnie chuckled.

"But it's true, and Ronnie knows it, too," O.A. said. "There are methods that are best for each season and each species. In fact, there are methods that work better on some lakes than others. You've just got to consider what will work at a given time and place."

Figure out how to catch the fish before you plan a fish fry.

"And you gotta know what you're capable of. Now, if you fellas will kindly excuse me, there's a Twinkie up there with my name on it," Ronnie said, heading for the counter.

"As ol' Buck Roland would say," O.A. said with theatrical flair, "analyze the situation carefully before taking action."

"I don't remember reading that in Buck's book," Frank said.

"Well, he said it. And there's one other thing," O.A. said. "Having a good attitude like our buddy Ronnie's doesn't hurt any either."

One size fits all . . . poorly

Frank had originally thought that fishing was something he could do on autopilot—just reel in the fish while enjoying good ol' Mother Nature. Now he's beginning to wonder if a few advanced degrees wouldn't help.

There are college graduates, as well as some veteran managers, who still don't appreciate the need to, as O.A. and Buck Roland would say, "analyze the situation carefully before taking action." They're convinced that the "tools" they learned in school fit all situations. And, of course, the most impressive way to solve a problem is by using the latest method or current fad.

Figure out how to catch the fish before you plan a fish fry.

■ ■ ■

Make sure the tool fits the problem.

Fishy Business

Ever hear about the guy who got an electric screwdriver for Christmas? The first thing he did was scamper around the house tightening every screw he could find. Next he did the same thing in the garage and to his two cars. Finally, with no screw left unscrewed, he filed grooves in the heads of every nail inside the house and out, and reached for his trusty screwdriver again.

This is kind of like Frank's boss, Big Jake, who reacts to almost every situation with the same tool—in his particular case, a loud bark. Other managers are seduced by what's in vogue. If reengineering is the current buzzword, that must be the magic bullet. If the winds shift and "teams" and "empowerment" are the fad, then we must quickly empower everyone in sight, team up, and charge ahead.

This is not to say that teams, empowerment, and reengineering are necessarily bad ideas. They can, in fact, be very good. But, like O.A. says, it all depends. Think about a team in which ol' Edgar is a member. Without much effort at all, he could bring everyone else down.

When it comes to teams, we must accept the fact that some people, including many of our most creative individuals, work better alone. Do you *really* think a team could have improved Michelangelo's painting on the Sistine Chapel ceiling?

CHAPTER 25

All About Buck

"Did I hear somebody mention the great Buck Roland?" Chuck said, coming over to join the group.

"O.A. was just telling me something Buck said, but I couldn't recall it from his book," Frank explained.

"Probably wasn't in the book," Chuck said, taking a seat. "Most likely it was just something he told you. Right, O.A.?"

"Oh yes, he said it plenty of times," O.A. said, smiling. "You've got to analyze—"

"—the situation before taking action," Chuck completed the adage.

"Still good advice," O.A. said.

"Wait a second," Frank said. "You guys knew Buck Roland?"

"Before he went off and became a famous tournament fisherman," Chuck said.

"He won a big tournament?" Frank asked.

"Actually, Buck won the first two national contests he entered, and topped it all off with a victory at the biggest bass tournament of that time," O.A. said. "Then he quit fishing competitively altogether."

Fishy Business

"What?" Frank couldn't understand how anyone at the top of his game could just give it up.

"That's Buck. But things worked out pretty well for him," O.A. said. "He went on to become a big-time TV fisherman. His show was far and away the most popular one for years. That was a long time before you took up fishing, of course."

"He was very successful," Chuck said, "but it never really changed him."

"Wow, I had no idea," Frank said. "Did you ever fish with him?"

"Oh, sure," Chuck said, "Buck's a great guy. And I'll tell you something, if he told you the bass were hitting a particular lure, you could take it to the bank."

Consider the source when taking advice.

"The way you guys are talkin' sounds like ol' Buck passed away," Ronnie said, wandering back with Twinkie in hand.

"He's still alive?" Frank was surprised.

"See, what'd I tell you." Ronnie pointed his Twinkie in Frank's direction.

"I'll introduce you two sometime," O.A. said.

"Great," Frank said. "By the way, O.A., when are *you and I* going to do a little fishing?"

"How's next Saturday sound, partner?"

"Done deal," Frank said.

"Bass or bluegills?" O.A. asked.

"Bluegills," Frank said. "I could use some more pointers on those guys."

"Great," O.A. said. "See you Saturday."

Let me check that out

Frank may not know it, but he's been awfully lucky up till now. Most everyone he has encountered on Lake Lindner knows a great deal about fishing and has been more than gracious in offering boatloads of worthwhile advice. Things would have undoubtedly been a good deal different if he had adopted Edgar as his mentor.

 Consider the source when taking advice.

■ ■ ■

Pick the right expert.

A good manager knows who the experts are in his or her organization and values the illumination they can shed on a given situation. Unfortunately, sometimes these bright lights are dimmed by a boss who doesn't know how to turn them on— or even find them.

Microsoft founder Bill Gates may have said it best, if not first: "I want to surround myself by the brightest people possible." Obviously, those kinds of people generally give the soundest advice. Makes sense, but some bosses are a little afraid to do this. Hey, one of those bright lights just may be brighter than he is.

On the other hand, be on the lookout for experts who aren't. A consultant who was looking into ways of improving scheduling at a plant was directed to Ralph. The boss who recommended him was sure that he was precisely the person who could help straighten things out. As he said, "We'd be lost without him." Sure sounded like Ralph was the guy to see.

The first hint of a problem came when the consultant noticed that Ralph wasn't overly busy. He began by asking him to detail his job responsibilities. He had no problem doing so,

Fishy Business

but when asked to go through a mock decision-making exercise—to do what he would normally do to determine the production schedule for the next time period—things bogged down.

Every few minutes, he excused himself (could have been too much coffee, who knows?). When he returned, though, Ralph seemed much more confident . . . until he was asked the next question. He would ponder, scratch his head, squirm, and excuse himself once again. This little charade went on for the next half hour.

Finally, the consultant could stand it no longer. The next time Ralph left, he jumped up and trailed him. He discovered that Ralph was heading not to the john, but to Jill. He conferred with his assistant on just about every facet of his decision making. It was easy to see who the real expert was. Ralph, of course, never told his superior of Jill's invaluable worth to the organization. Or had you already guessed that?

CHAPTER 26

Fish Sandwich

The following weekend, O.A. and Frank met at Bob's. When they purchased maggots, Bob went through the same ritual of spilling the squirmers into his hand to show off their vigor to the customers. Frank still wasn't keen on the custom.

"Anything else, O.A.?" Bob asked.

"How about some waxworms," he said.

More larval bait was trotted out for their inspection. Though slightly bigger, they were every bit as disgusting as the maggots. O.A. told Frank that on those occasions when bluegills wouldn't hit maggots, they would sometimes take waxworms.

"When the fishing gets really tough, some guys even fish a waxworm sandwich," O.A. said. Although it went against his better judgment, Frank asked what that was.

Bob supplied the answer. "That's where you thread a maggot, then a waxworm, and then another maggot on the same hook. Bluegills think it's yummy."

"Let's go fishing before I get sick," Frank said. Bob, smiling broadly, rang up the sale.

Fishy Business

Three days of rain had muddied Lake Lindner's usually clear water. O.A. knew that this could spell trouble trying to find and catch the shallow-water bluegills.

"Normally," O.A. explained, "we like to spot spawning bluegills before we try to catch them. If you don't actually see the fish guarding the eggs, you can still tell where they are by the nests."

"Nests?" Images of birds flapped through Frank's mind.

"Nests or beds—that's what you call them," O.A. said. "The male bluegill scoops out the nest by sweeping the lake bottom with his tail fin and body. After mating, the female takes off and he's left behind to baby-sit all by himself. When you can't see the beds, you have to search for places that *seem* good."

The fish aren't going to draw you a map.

"Since their nests are in shallow water, why not just fish near shore?" Frank asked logically.

"There's a lot of shoreline to fish here," O.A. said, with an expansive wave of his arm. "We could do that, and we might get lucky. Then, again, we might not."

"What about Andrews Bay?" Frank suggested. "Ronnie says he's caught some nice 'gills there."

"That is a good place to fish . . . in the summer," O.A. said. "But Andrews Bay is mucky, and bluegills make their nests in sand or gravel bottoms."

"The swim beach!" Frank said.

"The swim beach it is." O.A. was pleased that his partner had figured it out himself. Many years of fishing had taught him where the bluegills might be, but he knew the lesson would be more valuable if Frank was able to unlock the secret without his help. They headed for the beach.

113

James P. Ignizio and Bill Ignizio

"Rule one," O.A. said as they drifted in toward the beach, "is to keep away from the swimmers. For some reason, they don't like having us throw bobbers at them."

"Darn," Frank said, "you spoil all my fun."

Although O.A. often used a fly rod for spawning bluegills, he opted to stick with his spinning rod on this occasion. He knew from experience that he could usually catch more fish with the fly rod, but he also knew that Frank would be at a disadvantage. He would teach Frank how to use a fly rod, but that would come later.

Information, please

Frank made a guess about where the bluegills might be, and judging from O.A.'s reaction, it must have been a good one. The more you learn about fish and fishing, the "luckier" your guesses become.

 The fish aren't going to draw you a map.

■ ■ ■

You'll have to make lots of decisions based on incomplete information.

Frank, like all managers, often makes decisions based on incomplete information. In most of the books future managers read, decision making seems fairly cut-and-dried. The pages of their textbooks provide problems and case studies that usually offer all of the information needed to make nice, clean, academically acceptable decisions. Consequently, they all too often have unrealistic expectations about the ready availability of supporting information. In the "real world," this can result in "decision paralysis," an affliction that can have devastating results, as you'll see.

Fishy Business

While Bill Gates, mentioned earlier, is practically a household word, few have heard of Digital Research founder Gary Kildall, developer of the CPM operating system used for almost every early personal computer. CPM was, in fact, so dominant that most everyone conceded that part of the PC to Digital Research.

Then IBM got into the act. They had ignored personal computers at first, thinking of them as nothing but "toys." But after it became clear that they couldn't laugh PCs away, Big Blue put together their own PC—using parts and ideas from everyone else. The big selling point, of course, was those three letters on the case: I ... B ... M.

Once the package was designed, all IBM needed was the software. They decided to have Microsoft build the computer programming software and see if Digital Research might provide the even more important operating system.

When IBM came calling on Bill Gates, he was delighted to sign a contract to build programming languages for the new computer. But when they went to visit Gary Kildall, he wasn't home. They had to settle on talking with his wife. Meeting in Kildall's small Victorian home in Pacific Grove, they asked her to sign a nondisclosure agreement. Nothing else would happen until that detail was taken care of.

Gates had signed the same agreement without a moment's hesitation. Mrs. Kildall hesitated; she needed more information. She needed to talk to someone else. She didn't have all the facts at hand. The IBM representatives finally excused themselves.

IBM went back to Gates. How would *he* like to provide the operating system for IBM's personal computers? Would Bill Clinton like some fries with his hamburger? Would Madonna care for a little more exposure?

The rest, as they say, is history. The first operating system for the IBM PC was called MS-DOS, but boy, did it look and feel almost exactly like CPM. Microsoft went on to be the success story of the eighties. Digital Research? According to our search on the Internet, they got bought out by Novell, which promptly shut down the Monterey operation, closing the doors on this bit of personal-computer history.

CHAPTER 27

Fun at the Beach

The swim beach was almost deserted when O.A. and Frank arrived. Up near the parking lot, two teenage boys listlessly tossed a Frisbee around while waiting for teenage girls to show up. At the water's edge, a small child, under her mother's watchful eye, played in the sand. If tradition held, the rest of the merrymakers would join the early birds within the next hour or so.

O.A. positioned the boat well away from the sun-and-fun folks and anchored down. He used a small bobber and tied on a lead-weighted hook, or panfish spoon, as Bob called it. Since the beds were likely to be in shallow water, he didn't allow much line to extend below the bobber. Frank, sitting in the bow, rigged up in similar fashion, and it wasn't long before they were fishing.

The first bluegill of the day fell prey to O.A.'s renowned "waxworm sandwich." It proved to be a stunning success. The next three fish were also taken by O.A. Frank grudgingly rigged up a waxworm sandwich of his own and tossed it out. O.A. responded by catching two more males.

"Look at the orange bellies on those fish," O.A. said, showing Frank the brightly colored bluegills.

Frank pretended to admire the bull bluegills, but he would have preferred to look at some fish that *he* had caught. But to his credit, Frank didn't fuss about bad luck. Instead, he set down his rod and watched O.A. intently. His bait was positioned at about the same depth he had been fishing, and the line and bobber appeared the same, too. The panfish spoon was even the same color. What was he doing wrong?

O.A., who felt bad for Frank, knew what was wrong, but kept it to himself. He knew that the younger man simply had not been bluegill fishing very much, and was convinced that Frank would learn more by solving the problem himself. If he didn't figure it out soon, though, O.A. would step in and help.

"Could I see your panfish spoon for a second?" Frank asked.

O.A. tossed him a spoon similar to the one he was fishing. When Frank held both lures in his hand, the difference was readily apparent. O.A.'s panfish spoon was a good deal smaller than his. Everything Frank had been doing was the same, except for the critical matter of lure size. Frank couldn't believe he hadn't caught it earlier.

"It's not like you and Mike haven't mentioned that lure and hook size can be important," he said. "How could I be so dumb?"

The fish don't take it personally, so why should you?

"No harm done," O.A. said. "You figured it out in due time. But you really need to lighten up and treat yourself a little better, partner. Hey, you deserve it."

Frank wasn't sure if he had been chastised or compli-
mented. Since he liked the idea of a compliment better, he decided to take it that way. And while he was at it, he would
take O.A.'s advice and treat himself better . . . starting right
now.

I can't ever remember making a mistake

Frank's habit of beating up on himself for just about every mistake he makes is an easy one for a perfectionist like him to
fall into—but it doesn't help. Instead, he needs to relish his
progress rather than obsess on every little setback.

....

The fish don't take it personally, so why should you?

■ ■ ■

We all make mistakes.

....

We have a friend, a nice guy, who is deathly afraid of making mistakes. He won't consider investing in the stock market
since it might go down rather than up. He's too concerned about
divorce and the effect on his hypothetical children even to think
about marriage, and buying a house is out of the question. Hey,
it might catch fire. Whatever the reason for his quirks, he is
likely to end up with "decision paralysis," the same disease con-
tracted by folks who demand complete information.

This type of behavior is especially interesting in light of
the fact that so many managers who are afraid of making mistakes themselves demand no less than perfection from their subordinates. Frank's boss, Big Jake, may or may not have this
affliction. Whatever the case, he surely is a carrier, enthusias-
tically instilling fear in "his people" (as he calls them) who

118

spend more time trying to avoid mistakes than getting the job done.

If anyone deserved to beat themselves up it might be someone like Gary Kildall. And maybe he did. But what good would it do? The mistake was made, the damage done, but he still had his family, a nice business, and a home in Pacific Grove—the American dream for most of us.

So Bill Gates didn't make the same mistake, but what does he have to show for it? Yeah, we know, billions and billions of dollars, fame, power, and all that. You know, maybe this isn't such a good example after all.

Seriously, unless your mistake is terminal, you'll survive. Nobody—and this most definitely includes managers—can afford to wander through life in fear of mistakes. Besides, the surest way to fail is to live in fear of failing.

CHAPTER 28

The Artful Caster

The murky water made fishing for bedding bluegills slow. Still, using O.A.'s tip, Frank managed to catch a few nice fish. Best of all, he didn't even bother to compare the number of fish he caught with O.A.'s total.

"Ready for something a little different?" O.A. asked.

"Sure, what do you have in mind?"

"How about a little shore fishing?"

"Fine." Frank was game, but wondered why O.A. had bothered to take the boat out in the first place if he intended to fish from shore all along. Once on land, O.A. pulled out two fly rods he had brought along, quickly assembled them, and handed one to Frank.

"Ever use a fly rod?" he asked.

"No, but I've seen guys do it. Looks complicated," Frank said. "How long does it take to get the hang of it?"

"To get really good can take . . . oh, maybe a lifetime," O.A. said. "But to learn enough to catch fish with a fly rod takes maybe a half hour. We'll start you off with two basic casts. Some fishermen never go much beyond that. It's up to you."

Fishy Business

O.A. showed Frank the proper arm position for casting and then proceeded to demonstrate by moving the lightweight rod back, pausing long enough for the looping line to straighten out behind him. When he brought the rod forward at precisely the right moment, the line gracefully glided toward a feather-soft landing on the water.

"Beautiful," Frank said, admiring O.A.'s delicate touch with the long rod, "but what can a fly rod do that a spinning rod can't?" Frank asked.

"That's a great question," O.A. said. "It's not just a fancy way of fishing, I guarantee. When bluegills are on the beds, like today, it can be hard to catch them."

"Don't I know," Frank agreed.

"The fly rod allows you to catch fish that a spinning rod doesn't."

A good fishermen knows when to change rods.

"Is that because you don't use a bobber with a fly rod?" Frank asked.

"That's part of it," O.A. said. "A bobber splashing down tends to scare fish away. Think of it from their perspective: how would you like something the size of a Buick crashing down on you?"

"Good point, but you don't see a lot of guys using fly rods out here," Frank said, nodding in the direction of the lake.

"Most people equate fly-fishing with trout," O.A. said. "Since we don't have much in the way of trout hereabouts, they figure using a fly rod doesn't make sense. But you can catch other species this way.

"When bluegills are shallow, for instance, the fly rod really shines. In deep water, you might want to switch back to your spinning rod. It all depends on the situation."

O.A. found Frank an enthusiastic student of fly-fishing. Although he didn't become an instant expert, within twenty minutes the younger man was able to make a pretty good overhead cast and a serviceable if not graceful roll cast. O.A. promised him they would do some serious fly-fishing in the near future. Frank couldn't wait.

Time for a change?

O.A.'s lesson on knowing when to change from a spinning rod to a fly rod got Frank thinking about more than fishing. He suspects it may be time to make a change at work, too. We're willing to wager he'll do it.

 A good fisherman knows when to change rods.

■ ■ ■

A good manager knows when to change course.

Unfortunately, some managers fear change. After all, change can be risky, especially if it simply involves change for change's sake. Nevertheless, there may be an even bigger risk in refusing to act.

In the sixties and seventies, this country's automotive industry learned a costly lesson concerning the failure of recognizing the need to change. That's when those funny-looking little foreign cars started popping up on our shores. Glancing at the homely newcomers, Ford, GM, and Chrysler weren't concerned. Figuring the little puddle jumpers would fade away soon enough, they continued to build long, wide,

122

heavy, gas-guzzlers. And we all know how *that* story turned out.

While American industry *may* have learned a lesson about the need to change the way they design and build cars, there is an even more important need for change that is, for the most part, being ignored. This is the way most managers measure "productivity." Conventional wisdom has it that a productive plant or organization is one in which every machine and person is working at top speed. So "productivity" has become a proxy for "hustle." But that's only true if all the people and machines are working on the right thing, at the right time.

Instead of measuring how fast people and machines move, we should measure how well we achieve our main goal: making a profit. This won't happen until managers are willing to "change course."

Speaking of changing course, Frank has noticed an unsettling paradox at work. An increasing number of parts are missing their due dates, causing customers to look for other suppliers. This is happening in spite of all the new, automated machines that were purchased and installed throughout the firm. Big Jake, also feeling the heat, delivered his own blistering opinions in a recent meeting of the various plant managers.

Jake's opinions, usually broadcast in the high-decibel range, had become increasingly grating. What Frank once saw in Jake as forcefulness and leadership now seemed like petty bullying at best. Instead of conferring with his "team" to achieve success, Jake seemed to prefer tactics that called for harassment and intimidation. As a reward for laboring mindlessly and keeping your mouth shut, Jake allowed subordinates to watch as he claimed any accolades that happened to stray even remotely in his direction. And, all the while, production dropped.

While early indications pointed in the direction of downsizing and yet more automation, Frank was no longer convinced that this was the answer to his company's ills. He certainly doesn't feel that "lazy" workers are the cause of the problems.

In fact, it seems as though both management and labor are working harder and longer. Yet they continue to fall behind. How can this be?

It may be time to send for some outside help . . . with or without Big Jake's approval—or knowledge. Frank thinks he knows just the person to call.

CHAPTER 29

The Awful Caster

That evening, as O.A. put his gear away, he reflected on Frank's enthusiasm for fly-fishing. The way he had picked it up was in stark contrast to another fisherman he had tutored several years ago.

Edgar, a card-carrying sourpuss if there ever was one, had observed O.A. fishing for bass with a fly rod. When O.A. hooked a large fish, Edgar thought this might be the solution he had been looking for so long. If only O.A. would show him the "secret" of the long rod, could also catch fish after fish.

O.A. was more than a little surprised when Edgar approached him and asked for a few lessons. Up to that point, he doubted if the man had said more than a handful of words to him in all the years he had known him. It didn't matter; O.A. turned nobody away who asked him for fishing advice.

He pointed Edgar in the direction of an inexpensive fly rod, helped him select line, and gave him several flies he had tied himself. After demonstrating the proper casting procedure, Edgar began whipping the rod through the air as though he were beating a rug. He shot his arm back and forth so quickly a series of wind knots developed in the fly line's leader.

"Uh, Edgar," O.A. said, "if you could stop waving that thing around for just a second, I'd like to point something out."

"What?" Edgar said, mopping his brow with a blue-and-white handkerchief.

"You notice a cracking sound while you were casting the fly rod?"

"Yeah, I guess so," Edgar said.

"Well, that's caused by the speed your line is traveling. Those little snap, crackle, and pops you hear are actually your line breaking the sound barrier."

"Not good?" Edgar asked, looking at the knotty line.

It's how well you cast, not how fast.

"I'm afraid not. We'll have to slow down your cast a little," O.A. suggested.

O.A. had tried, but he couldn't get Edgar to change his fast-motion cast. Other lessons followed, but his improvement was as slow as his casting motion was fast. Edgar seemed to think that more casts would result in more fish. It *seemed* logical. To Edgar at least.

O.A. contrasted his experience with poor contrary ol' Edgar to Frank. Sure, Frank was sometimes impatient to learn it all overnight and often a tad too competitive for his own good. But O.A. felt he understood Frank. In fact, as he had reflected on more than one occasion, Frank reminded O.A. of himself at that age. The important point was that Frank listened and was willing to change. O.A. liked that.

Forty *years, and only* ten *commandments?*

Whatever else you may say about Edgar, you certainly can't fault his work ethic. The man felt the harder and faster he fished, the better he would fish. Like many others, he confused appearances with results.

It's how well you cast, not how fast.

■　■　■

Measure the outcome, not just the effort.

Unfortunately, many organizations confuse effort with outcome. Effort, after all, is easier to measure. You can measure how many parts an hour a worker processes, how many words a typist types, how many rounds a soldier fires, or how many students graduate college. But in a world that sometimes seems to be dominated by bean counters, we often wind up counting the wrong beans.

We've touched on this notion in the previous chapter; so let's be a little more precise in this one. It will help if we first look at the way in which most companies measure performance.

At one unnamed organization, the "productivity" of software developers was measured by the number of lines of computer code they generated per day. The more lines of code, the more productive the programmer. Or so it was thought. Instead of rewarding those who were creative enough to use fewer lines of code to accomplish a given task, they were chastised for being less productive.

Here's a related story we'll share—if you promise not to tell anyone. More than twenty years ago, I was given an assignment by the U.S. Army to develop a method that would deploy air-defense missile radars. I completed the task by developing a new method that some say outperformed anything else in existence—then or now.

At that time, computer programs that implemented such methods were stored as punched cards—the old "IBM cards" you may have seen in museums. Pleased as punch with my effort, I submitted a small stack (about three inches thick) of cards, held together with a few rubber bands, along with the final report.

I explained that this method would take only a few minutes to run for their biggest problem. At that time, other methods took days, most often with inferior results.

The military's response? Dismay. They were convinced that a problem that complex couldn't be solved that fast, particularly with so few lines of computer code. It made no difference that program testing had conclusively demonstrated that it worked, beating the competition soundly.

In frustration, I gathered several hundred punched cards lying around the office (it didn't matter what purpose they were designed for) and slipped them into my small deck. In no time at all, my three inches of cards suddenly grew to several boxes. Then, for good measure, I inserted a few lines of code that served to bypass all the unnecessary cards and cycle for an hour or so longer than necessary before spitting out the answer.

You've probably guessed the result. The army was delighted that I had finally "got it right."

A similar philosophy exists at Frank's company. Yet, unless it supports, rather than hurts, your ultimate goal, *more* is not necessarily *better.*

CHAPTER 30

Spare the Rods and
Spoil the Fisherman

With a little spare time on his hands after work, Frank checked out his growing collection of rods and reels. He replaced line wherever needed and oiled the reels. When he first began fishing, maintenance had gone much faster with only a single rod and reel. He remembered thinking at the time how strange it was that some fishermen felt the need for so many different outfits. After all, you can only fish one rod at a time.

Bob had set him straight on that point. "Those guys don't haul around a boatload of rods for their health," he said. "There's a reason for each and every rod they use."

Frank found that a little hard to swallow. Bob was not dissuaded, and proceeded to show Frank the flaw in his reasoning.

"That's a pretty good little outfit you have there, right?" Bob said, pointing to Frank's rod and reel.

"It better be. I bought it from you."

"That means it's great. Remember when you came in here and said you were starting out fishing, and I suggested that spincast outfit?"

"Right," Frank said, not seeing quite where Bob was heading.

"Well, it is a good outfit . . . for a beginner. There'll come a time, though, when you'll want to make sure your casts are right on the money," Bob said.

"And that can only be done with a more expensive outfit?"

"Not necessarily," Bob said, "but you'll find that you can cast a lot more accurately with a spinning outfit because of the way the reel's designed."

Frank thought it was sales hype at the time, but he had to admit that his casts could stand a little improvement. Time had proven Bob correct. Less than a month later, he purchased his first spinning outfit. Not long afterward, he bought a bait-casting rod and reel.

One rod can't do it all.

Looking back, he realized that fishing different outfits was a lot like carrying several clubs in your golf bag. The game was infinitely easier when the club suited the shot you faced.

Now Frank looked at the fly rod O.A. had loaned him and wondered if he'd ever find the need to buy more than one of those. He already knew the answer to that question.

Did you get the number of that plane?

When Frank first took up fishing he had some high hopes and grand expectations. He's now gotten to the point where he realizes that some of those expectations were naive—like thinking that one rod and reel would take care of all his fishing needs. Some managers never learn that lesson, and their unrealistic expectations can do considerable damage. Unless, of course, you're as clever as Chuck Yeager.

Fishy Business

One rod can't do it all.

■ ■ ■

Beware of unrealistic expectations.

Yeager, in his autobiography, tells a story that clearly illustrates problems associated with unrealistic expectations. Then-Colonel Yeager, the original man with "the right stuff," found himself in Vietnam in the mid-sixties. In charge of the 405th Fighter Wing, composed of five squadrons scattered all over Southeast Asia, he still managed to squeeze in 127 combat missions. As if fighting a war and overseeing five squadrons weren't enough, Yeager's commanding officer sometimes seemed like an even bigger problem.

To say that Yeager's boss was a stickler for details would be a gross understatement. Attention to details, as we've mentioned before, can help ensure a company's success. As with most anything, however, there has to be a balance. Yeager's boss apparently lost sight of this fact—at least as Yeager tells the story.

Every airplane in Yeager's wing was due for maintenance according to a rigid schedule that called for matching the tail number of the plane to a due date. This meant that Yeager had to predict—a month in advance and in the middle of a war— just when each plane would need maintenance. And it didn't matter to his boss whether the plane got shot up or down.

To make sure that his orders were being followed to the letter, Yeager's commanding officer had his staff car positioned by the runway while he personally checked off the tail numbers of each airplane as they paraded past. When the general carefully compared each tail number with his master list, they'd damn well better match up.

Yeager found the inflexible and unrealistic maintenance scheme frustrating, to say the least. He felt that this gigantic waste of time and effort could and should have been directed toward far more productive matters. But the ace fighter pilot hadn't become the first person to break the speed of sound without some effective decision-making skills. So he came up with a unique solution.

After a plane had been checked off by the general, it headed back to the hangar. There, Yeager's people quickly painted over the tail number and sent it back to be viewed again. This meant that airplane number 357, shot out of the sky a week earlier, still came cruising past the general's staff car. Clearly, the general's unrealistic expectations had led to silly rules which, like the sound barrier, begged to be broken.

Many managers tend to think like Yeager's boss, basing their hopes on unrealistic expectations reinforced by silly policies and procedures. Anyone who believes that reengineering, teams, total quality control, strategic planning, surfing the Himalayas—or even fishing—will solve all their problems has missed the point.

CHAPTER 31

Wilson River Runs Through It

Two weeks after their outing for spawning bluegills found Frank and O.A. wading the winding Wilson River, noted for its plentiful population of rainbow trout. When O.A. had proposed the weekend trip, Frank accepted in a flash. He was excited at the prospect of fishing out of state for the first time.

Looking downstream, Frank watched O.A., silhouetted against the morning sun, send the tapered fly line back in a tight loop. Then, using a method he called a "double haul," he pulled down on the line with his left hand as the rod moved forward. At just the right moment, he released the line, causing it to shoot out, making for a longer cast. Frank enjoyed watching the maneuver, but was far from perfecting it himself.

A smattering of small yellow flowers lined the opposite bank and tall grass bordered the river's near side. Insects flitted near the flowers and above the water's surface. If you looked hard, you could see a dimple here and there on the water's surface. Trout were feeding!

Earlier that morning, O.A. had pointed out several ant mounds onshore. He showed Frank some of the ant-shaped flies he had brought along.

"Sometimes when trout are feeding on ants, they'll slurp down just about anything that approximates the shape of an ant. Other days they're picky; it all depends. There are over seven hundred species of ants in North America," he explained.

"Let's hope we don't have to try them all," Frank said, shaking his head. The fish were selective on this day, but not impossibly so. They simply wanted a floating cinnamon-colored size fourteen ant. Luckily for Frank, O.A. had them.

Peering through his polarized sunglasses, Frank could make out rocks beneath the water's surface. He moved slowly for two reasons: first, he would cast toward the rocks, and second, he didn't want to trip over them.

Polarized sunglasses let you see the fish's world.

O.A. had explained that trout used the rocks as feeding stations. "They may not be the most intelligent creatures on earth," he said, "but they know enough to come in out of the current. By nestling behind a rock, they wait for the current to bring their food to them."

Fish often hold near specific features.

Frank found on-the-stream conditions a little more difficult to contend with than casting from his backyard or on peaceful Lake Lindner. He muffed several casts and was not nearly as artistic in his technique as O.A. No matter, it was an invigorating experience, and he knew he would try it again.

O.A. caught two trout within an hour, the largest measuring a little over a foot long, while Frank had a fish take a swipe at one of his ant flies. Then he saw it. At first, it looked like a small log. But logs don't float in place on a fast-flowing stream.

He squinted his eyes, and it was still there behind a large, almost perfectly round rock. It was a very big trout. Yet, since he had seen the fish, he knew it probably saw him, too. Generally, that meant it wouldn't hit.

Still, Frank couldn't pass it up. He stood still for over a minute, which at that moment seemed like a long, long time. Then he cast out his ant and let it drift down toward the fish. The big trout didn't hesitate; it slurped in the fly immediately.

Frank set the hook and was startled by the force the fish exerted. It wasn't nearly as large as the carp he had caught on Circle Creek. Yet it fought like the devil! No wonder O.A. had said there's nothing like trying to land a decent fish with a fly rod.

The line unexpectedly went limp, and so did Frank's spirits . . . but only momentarily. He hadn't done anything wrong. The powerful fish had managed to snap the thin line (or tippet). Score one for the trout. But, Frank thought with a smile, the day had only begun.

Haven't we seen this guy before?

Polarized sunglasses are a great aid to almost any kind of fishing. It's like opening a window into the fish's world, allowing you to see things you might otherwise miss. Similar in some ways to hiring a good consultant.

Polarized sunglasses let you see the fish's world.

■ ■ ■

A good consultant sees things you might miss.

Not all sunglasses allow you to see beneath the water's reflective surface. Similarly, not all consultants consistently produce positive results. When you find one that does, however, the results can bring about dramatic improvements.

A consultant has an important advantage over those directly involved in the problem to be solved. Being an outsider, he or she will have a different perspective on things. A competent consultant can often see things others miss. One problem any *good* consultant looks for are bottlenecks. As mentioned earlier, you will often find an organization's experts at the bottlenecks.

Another reason for identifying bottlenecks is to identify and explain problems. If you want to process matters faster, for example, you could off-load some of your expert's workload by bringing in help of some kind. Trying to "hurry things up" *behind* the bottleneck is obviously not a solution to the problem. Too often, though, that is the "solution" that is implemented.

Fish often hold near specific features.

■ ■ ■

Your problems pile up at your bottlenecks.

Fishy Business

A way to find bottlenecks on a plant floor is to look for a work pileup, or in-process inventory, directly behind it. The machine, test center, lab, or inspector directly in front of that pile is unable to process things fast enough to keep up with input. This means that the machines and people behind the bottleneck have two choices: slow down and wait, or continue on, causing the unfinished piles of work behind the bottleneck to just grow higher.

In such cases, it may be better to let the machines and people feeding the bottleneck go idle. But, as we have discussed earlier, managers find it hard to believe that people and machines apparently doing "nothing" may actually be helping (to some degree, at least) the problem. In too many cases, the workers and machines are kept running—making the problem worse.

Our friend Frank has precisely this problem. Using conventional wisdom, and traditional measures of productivity, he and all the other plant-floor managers at his firm are unable to get their products out on time. Customers are angry, the salespeople are going nuts, and everyone in the front office is telling the people in manufacturing to "just work harder." But working harder is not the same as working smarter.

Unlike the other floor managers, Frank has sought outside help. Bringing in one of his old professors, Henry (just call me Hank) Nichols, they were able to quickly identify the bottlenecks on the QRT500 product line—one of the lines Frank is responsible for. The next step is to initiate a new, and controversial, solution—one that will actually slow down some machines and people rather than speed them up.

Frank hopes that Big Jake won't hear about this until they can prove that the approach works. He knows all too well that Jake will tolerate no deviations from his orders. Nevertheless, Frank has decided to court professional disaster and follow Hank's advice. If things go as planned, the problems on the QRT500 line should be solved, and the same approach could be used elsewhere.

CHAPTER 32

Mike Spills the Bass

"Wow, nice fish!" Ellen said as she entered Bob's Bait and Tackle and caught sight of the huge photograph hanging on the wall. Frank couldn't believe the blowup showing him holding his whopper carp was still on display.

"When are you going to take that thing down?" he asked Bob.

"You gotta be kidding," Bob said, looking genuinely shocked. "That picture is a real attention getter. I think a lot of customers come in just to look at it."

"I'm sure," Frank said.

"Say, Frank, are you going to sign up for the twenty-second annual 'Bob's Buddy Bassin' Tournament?'" Bob asked.

"I had thought about it," he said, "but O.A. is fishing with Ronnie, and just about everybody else already has a partner."

"I don't," Ellen said.

"Hey, that's a great idea," Frank said. "Sign us up, Bob."

Frank and Ellen used the rest of the day to tune up for the tournament. Ellen's casts were on the money, as usual, and Frank was able to select spots that gave up a fish or at least a nibble. They might not win, but they wouldn't embarrass themselves.

"Hey, sport, how's it going?" a familiar voice called out.

"Why it's Mike, my old carpin' buddy," Frank told Ellen.

"Hi, Mike," Ellen called out. "Nice picture you took of Frank."

"Why, thank you," Mike said, rowing over to Frank's boat. "I'm glad that you appreciate my photographic prowess."

"Right," Frank said. "How are they hitting for you?"

"Pretty good," Mike said, "but O.A. and Ronnie are really pounding the bass down in Andrews Bay off the east shore."

"Will you be fishing the tournament next weekend?" Ellen asked.

"No, I can't make it," Mike said. They talked for a few minutes more before parting company.

"Well, we won't have to worry about Mike," Ellen said.

"What do you mean?"

"That's one less person we have to beat," she said confidently.

"Wait a second—I just thought of something," Frank said.

"What's that?" Ellen asked.

"I just realized that Mike tipped us off to the spot where O.A. and Ronnie will most likely be fishing during the tournament."

"The bass may not even be hitting there next weekend," Ellen said.

"No, but I think we should avoid Andrews Bay, anyhow," Frank said.

Cheating won't make you a better angler.

"Absolutely," Ellen agreed. That matter was settled, and Frank felt good about it. He was competitive, but he would play by the rules.

James P. Ignizio and Bill Ignizio

If it's not right, it's wrong

Frank and Ellen were given the opportunity to use some important inside knowledge—namely the precise spot at which their most serious competition would likely be fishing the day of the tournament. Mike's tip was an innocent slip of the tongue, and they certainly hadn't sought it. Still, making use of it wouldn't be right.

In competitive fishing, it's called sportsmanship. In business, it's called ethics by some, and naïveté by others. Our hopelessly old-fashioned parents and grandparents simply called it honesty.

In fishing, cheating is most likely to occur in big-money tournaments, where the stakes are high. So, you cheat a little and win a lot? Big deal, nobody gets hurt.

The truth, of course, is that cheating doesn't make you a better fisherman. And think of what could happen if you are found out. For those who don't care about either of these consequences, there's little that can be said or done to change their outlook.

 Cheating won't make you a better angler.

■ ■ ■

Cheating won't make you a better manager—or person.

As newspaper headlines constantly remind us, there are plenty of opportunities to cheat in business. A junior executive cheats a little, makes millions of dollars before getting caught and winding up in prison. While idling away a few years in a plush cell for nonviolent offenders, he might even find the time to write a best-selling book about his misdeeds.

Fishy Business

Big Jake isn't involved in illegal deals, but he certainly thinks nothing of taking credit for Frank's ideas. So far, like some white-collar crooks, he has been handsomely rewarded for this little "indiscretion." And he shows no sign of changing his ways.

Why then should a manager play fair? Only one reason we can think of: because it's the right thing to do.

CHAPTER 33

Would You Like Me to Charge That?

More than forty teams had entered Bob's twenty-second annual buddy bass-fishing tournament. Frank and Ellen knew some of the competitors, but many others were unfamiliar to them. A dense fog made Bob especially cautious in beginning the competition. Using a bullhorn, he quickly reviewed the rules and told the fishermen that the start would be staggered. That way, he explained, they could avoid all taking off at once and smashing into each other before they even began.

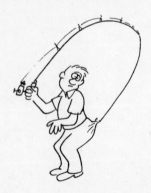

Fishy Business

Things went smoothly, with O.A. and Ronnie, last year's champions, moving out first. It looked to Frank as though O.A. was motoring directly for Andrews Bay. Frank and Ellen had drawn thirty-eighth place and had to wait their turn patiently.

As Frank squinted through the fog, he noticed the unlikely team of Edgar and Mark, the troller Ronnie had introduced to him several weeks ago. He waved in their direction and a smiling Mark waved back. Frank wasn't certain, but Edgar may have nodded his head in acknowledgment.

"Ol' Edgar must be feeling sprightly this morning," he said to Ellen.

"What's that?" she asked.

"I'm just surprised Edgar found a partner who could put up with him," Frank said. "I'll explain as we run to our spot . . . if nobody else has already taken it."

Unfortunately for Frank and Ellen, the spot where they had caught two bass the previous weekend was occupied by Chuck and Art. Chuck waved as Frank dejectedly putted on to look for another spot.

The spot Chuck had selected had always been good to him. He had no idea that it had also produced well for Frank and Ellen. Working the woody shoreline cover in the stiff wind wasn't easy, but Chuck felt he was up to it. And he was, but his battery wasn't.

Thinking he had prepared about as well as possible, Chuck had forgotten one crucial item: charging the battery that ran the electric trolling motor. The mistake proved costly, forcing him to resort to the oars to set up casts. This meant that he wasn't able to cast as much or fish as effortlessly as he could have with the trolling motor.

 Even the best angler makes a mistake now and then.

"I can't believe I did that," Chuck said, turning to Art. "I just may have lost the tournament for us."

"So, next year I'll be in charge of charging the battery," Art said. "In the meantime, let's fish and have some fun."

Chuck was relieved that Art took it so well. Still, he felt awfully bad about his goof.

Convoys? We don't need no stinking convoys!

Poor Chuck may have fouled things up, but he was big enough to admit his error. Some managers can't bring themselves to do that. One of the most notorious cases we've heard of involves U.S. Navy brass and the German U-boat "problem."

Even the best angler makes a mistake now and then.

■ ■ ■

Not admitting a mistake may be an even bigger mistake.

During the first six months after the United States entered World War II, U-boats destroyed nearly six hundred ships, the equivalent of half the American merchant ships afloat at the time. Winston Churchill was convinced that American unpreparedness and incompetence (in dealing with U-boats) was a far greater threat to the Allied effort than any other factor of the war. Historians seem to agree.

Through a series of bloody trials and errors, the British learned that the only way to safeguard the passage of merchant ships was by means of large convoys, with each convoy protected by a complement of fighting escorts. British academicians (known as "operational researchers") even devised a way to configure each convoy and determine where to place each escort vessel so as to maximize the probability of the entire convoy making it safely across the Atlantic. Churchill transmitted this information to Roosevelt, who passed it on to the commander in chief of the U.S. Atlantic Fleet. He, in turn, presented it to his staff.

The staff, often referring to sentiments *dating back to the War of 1812,* weren't much interested in this "limey" scheme. Our navy decided to keep on doing the same thing, and continued attempting to sneak unprotected ships across the Atlantic a few at a time, or in a long and unprotected line akin to a wagon train snaking its way across the prairie. The results of the scheme were disastrous to the Americans.

Despite heavy losses, the navy refused to abandon the plan. "Stealth" would continue to be the order of the day. Besides, who could spare fighting ships to baby-sit the merchant fleet when they might be needed for some epic sea battles?

Our stealth policy did little to help the British. Each month approximately 750,000 tons of much-needed equipment was sent to the bottom of the North Atlantic by U-boats. Worse yet, the human cost was staggering—and the merchant marines were close to rebellion.

Ultimately, the navy brass conceded—grudgingly. Convoys were initiated and the situation turned in favor of the Allies. In the interim, the cost of simply failing to admit a mistake had been devastating.

CHAPTER 34

The Joy of Doing Nothing

The night before the tournament Frank and Ellen had decided on five spots they were confident would yield bass. As backups, they came up with a dozen more that might give up a fish or two. They had done well the preceding weekend, but this was an entirely different situation. Not only were there forty other teams out on the lake searching for bass, but a dreaded cold front had passed through. The hungry bass had lost their appetite, making fishing a trial.

"Is it my imagination," Frank said, "or are all of our prime locations taken?"

"That's about the size of it," Ellen said. What she didn't say was that it was beginning to look like all the fallback spots were also occupied by other competitors. While the rules allowed other boats to fish the same general area, Frank and Ellen had already decided to give other anglers a wide berth.

"Ellen, check out Matousek Bay," Frank said.

Peering through binoculars, she saw that this little pocket of water seemed empty—until a boat headed in that direction. Then, for whatever reason, it headed back out of the bay and continued down the shoreline.

Fishy Business

"Go for it," Ellen said. Running full throttle, Frank made waves for Matousek Bay. Their ecstasy soon turned to agony as they plied just about every trick in their arsenal. The cold front had done its damage, effectively shutting the mouth of every bass in the bay. Ellen and Frank didn't give up, however, and kept trying new baits and tactics. Nothing worked.

"That's it!" Ellen said after an hour of fruitless fishing.

"That's what?" Frank asked.

"We'll do nothing," she said, tying on a small jig.

"Fine with me. I'm hungry anyhow. You bring any baloney sandwiches?" Frank paused. "Hey, maybe baloney would do it."

"Live bait's not allowed," Ellen reminded him.

"Baloney's pretty dead," Frank corrected.

Ellen's plan was to cast out a lightweight jig and crawl it back so slowly you could feel your hair growing, as O.A. would say. After an hour of crawling, Frank was rewarded with an almost imperceptible bump.

"Wow, what excitement," he said. "I think I almost felt a fish hit my jig."

"That's a good sign," Ellen said, ignoring the obvious sarcasm. She tied on a brown weightless worm and tossed it out. Although Frank was working his jig very slowly, Ellen had gone him one better. She simply let the worm lie on the lake bottom.

Sometimes the best action is no action.

"You ever going to bring that thing in?" Frank asked after she had sat there with rod in hand for more than fifteen minutes.

"Uh-huh," she said, jerking back on the rod. A bass had finally taken the bait.

"You are a genius!" Frank said, grabbing the net.

"That's what I keep telling you," Ellen agreed.

James P. Ignizio and Bill Ignizio

When in trouble or in doubt, don't just stand there, run and shout!

At first it looked as though Frank and Ellen were careening around Lake Lindner like a couple of drunken sailors. Then, when they finally found a spot they could fish, they seemed to go into hibernation. And what about Ellen's tactic of allowing the artificial worm to lie motionless on the lake bottom? What kind of plan is that?

Appearances can be deceiving. On this particular day this was probably the best approach they could have taken. The run-and-gun bass fishermen may have felt more active, but they weren't nearly as effective. Outside of giving their outboard motors a workout, the shoot-and-scoot boys accomplished little.

 Sometimes the best action is no action.

■ ■ ■

There are times when it's best to do nothing.

Sometimes it's best just to sit back and draw a few breaths before rushing into the fray. Sometimes it's best not to even enter it. While there's no doubt that response time is a major factor in business, you'd better draw a clear distinction between fast responses and good responses—or even the need to respond.

If you've suffered under impatient bosses, you may have firsthand knowledge of this. One such boss, Pete, reminded his employees of a pot of popcorn sitting on a hot stove. It seemed that every fifteen minutes or so he would pop over and demand an immediate change to whatever they might be working on at the time. Usually, about an hour or so later, he would pop back, telling everyone to forget about the change. He had come up with an even better idea; so get cracking on it!

It didn't take long before Pete's subordinates realized that there was but one way to live with him. They just did what *they* thought was right. When Pete rushed in, everyone listened, agreed to make the change, and then went on doing what they had been doing all along.

In this way, they kept their sanity, and got the job done right. In the meantime, Popcorn Pete was free to go running about like the proverbial chicken with its head cut off.

The world's favorite soft drink provides yet another example of a situation where doing nothing would have been the best course of action. Reacting to a problem that evidently didn't exist, the beverage manufacturer changed the formula for their longtime moneymaker. But the new cola fared poorly, and the company was forced to bring back the original drink. They should have paused long and hard before even thinking about tampering with the classic recipe of the fizzy drink once touted as the "pause that refreshes."

CHAPTER 35

Weight a Minute

After more than three hours of hard fishing, Frank and Ellen had taken a total of two bass. Should they stay in Matousek Bay and continue with the "do-nothing" method of letting the bait lie on the lake bottom or take off for greener pastures (make that bluer waters)? For better or worse, they opted to stay put.

Frank sensed rather than felt a nibble. He reeled in slack line and set the hook with a strong wrist snap. The fish didn't put up much of a fight.

"I think I have a baby bass on the line," he told Ellen as he easily cranked the fish in. To their mutual surprise the fish actually made the required length limit. Although a little embarrassed at his puny trophy, Frank added the bass to the other two in the portable livewell.

"I hate to tell you this, Frank," Ellen said, "but time's almost up. We'd better head back to weigh in our fish."

"Away we go," Frank said, revving up the outboard.

Most of the other competitors were already there when Frank and Ellen arrived. He shut down the outboard and used the electric motor to cruise over to O.A. and Ronnie.

Fishy Business

"How'd you guys do?" Frank asked.

"Five fish," Ronnie said. "It was tough fishin' out there."

Frank was a little disappointed that O.A. and Ronnie had outfished them, but he was not crestfallen. As he sat waiting to weigh in his fish, he heard several other competitors complaining that they hadn't caught a single bass. At least they hadn't been skunked.

The weigh-in went quickly, as many boats had no fish to register. Edgar and Mark had caught only two fish, but one— a four-pounder—was the biggest of the day. O.A. and Ronnie's five bass were surprisingly small, but their total weight beat Edgar and Mark's by a good pound, putting them in first place—for the moment.

Finally, Frank and Ellen weighed in their three fish. Bob announced the total weight and the assembled anglers and onlookers applauded. They had won the tournament by two ounces!

When conditions are tough, fishing is hard for everyone.

Bob, whose voice had settled comfortably into a carnival barker cadence, announced: "Time for the awarding of plaques, ladies and gentlemen. In third place, the team of Edgar and Mark."

As Bob handed each man a small plaque, Frank saw something very unusual. The others saw it, too. Edgar was smiling. Holding the little plaque as though it were a precious jewel, he headed over to O.A. and shook his hand vigorously.

"I caught my bass on a fly rod," Edgar said. "I guess your lessons paid off after all."

"In second place, Ronnie and O.A.," Bob called out. "Now, don't feel sorry for them, ladies and gentlemen. These guys have won first place in this tournament five times already."

When Frank and Ellen walked up to accept their trophy, they found it difficult to believe that they had really won. They looked in O.A.'s direction and saw him smiling broadly. Ronnie, standing beside him, gave a thumbs-up gesture while Edgar pumped a fist in the air in their honor.

It was a day neither of them would forget.

Right data, wrong interpretation

Frank and Ellen didn't think they had a chance to win the big tournament, or even place. The weather was rotten, the bass were uncooperative, and they hadn't caught enough fish to make much of a showing—or so they thought. What they failed to consider was that conditions were bad for everyone.

When conditions are tough, fishing is hard for everyone.

■ ■ ■

It's all relative.

Some managers react the same way. Sales last year may have hit a new company high. But this year they may have "fallen" by half. When you put it that way, it sure sounds like things are bad, and that someone must have failed. The "solution" might well be big changes in the offing and heads rolling.

But if your competitors have experienced the same falloff, or worse, have you really failed? If you've actually made the best of a bad situation, it may not be time to make drastic changes—or to even change course.

As O.A. is so fond of saying, "It all depends." There are times, of course, when changes are necessary. But it makes no sense to penalize individuals who have done relatively well under difficult and unforeseen circumstances. If you've just experienced an extraordinarily lousy year, you'll only hurt yourself and your company by looking upon a temporary setback as a "loss."

One of the reasons things are going downhill at Frank's company concerns just such a lack of perspective. A few years ago, orders for several of their products dropped because of a decline in worldwide demand. Although little could be done about the situation, the VP of sales went through the roof. Pointing to the sharp downturn in "his" sales, he placed the blame squarely on production. Figuring that if you make more, you'll sell more, he saw to it that production was stepped up. So, new automated machines were bought, work teams were formed, action management courses were implemented, and a sense of urgency resounded throughout the entire firm.

The immediate result was a huge amount of products that were popular a year or so earlier, but were now considered obsolete by most of their customers. But the ultimate result has been a shocking reduction in products being sent out the door. The vice president would have served his company, his customers, and his employees better by checking conditions all over the "lake" before insisting on the wrong response.

CHAPTER 36

Did You Ever Have to
Make Up Your Mind?

It had been three weeks since Frank and Ellen had won the big tournament. Today, they were fishing purely for pleasure.

"What are you going to do, Frank?" Ellen asked.

"I'm sorry, what did you say?" Frank looked up from rummaging through the tackle box.

"Are you going to use a spinnerbait or a buzzbait? Have you made up your mind yet?"

Looking out over the weedy bay, Frank said: "You're absolutely right. I've got to make up my mind, and I just did. I'm going with a weedless popper."

Choosing the right lure can be hard.

"Not a bad idea," Ellen said, casting out a spoon.

Fishy Business

The gentle plop of Frank's weedless soft-plastic popper touching down near a clump of cattails alerted a huge bass that something good was in the vicinity. It swam over to investigate. Frank would be ready when it snapped up the lure.

Decision time

Frank's decision to use the rubber popper didn't come easily. This may have been because a much more important decision was weighing on his mind at the time. Should he clear the air once and for all with Big Jake? And was he willing to accept the likely consequences?

 Choosing the right lure can be hard.

■ ■ ■

Making the right decision can be difficult.

Frank considered his options. He could ignore the fact that Hank's advice regarding the QRT500 production line had been right on, and he could let Big Jake continue with business as usual. Or he could confront Jake with the stunning results of the trial run he and Ed Bates had covertly implemented. Frank smiled to himself as he thought back to Bates's expression when he first confronted him with Hank's radical plan.

"You and Hank want to do *what?*" Bates seemed to be in shock.

As Frank patiently explained his idea, Bates held up a hand as a symbol to stop. Frank was afraid he had offended the man.

"I can't believe you're willing to risk carrying this out," Bates said.

"Oh, I am," Frank said, "but I can certainly understand if you want no part of it."

Bates simply chuckled. Frank wasn't sure what he said to cause this reaction.

"Frank, I'm not laughing at *you*," Bates explained. "It's just that I had a similar idea. Not as detailed and well thought out maybe, but along the same lines."

Leading him to his office, Bates showed Frank notes for improvements he had made over the last several months. Frank was impressed—and pleased. Much of what Ed was already doing provided the support needed to implement Hank's master plan—even quicker than they had thought possible. It was obvious that he and Hank hadn't been the only ones who realized that Jake's tactics were wrongheaded.

Any manager in his right mind should have been able to see that Jake's "look busy at all costs" policy was a miserable failure. On the other hand, who said Jake was in his right mind? If Jake was true to form, he would probably ignore the facts and focus on Frank's insubordination.

If so, Frank didn't care to fish in Big Jake's pond any longer. There was no malice in Frank's decision, just conviction. It simply made no sense to continue on the path that he was treading at work. It was time to act.

CHAPTER 37

The Big One That Didn't Get Away

Frank held up the largest bass he had ever caught—in fact, the largest bass he had ever seen. Ellen didn't have to tell him to smile as she snapped off a couple of pictures before the fish was released.

"You did it, Frank," Ellen said. "That's the fish of a life-time."

When they got back to Bob's Bait and Tackle, he saw that Ronnie and Mike were there. Ellen excitedly told them about the huge bass he had just caught, and they congratulated him.

"Thanks, guys," Frank said sincerely.

"For what? Hey, you caught that fish all by your lonesome, ol' buddy," Ronnie said.

"That's right, sport," Mike agreed. "After all, we weren't in the boat with you."

"Oh, yes you were," Frank said. "Yes, you were."

Give credit where it's due.

Gunfight at the O.A. Corral

The afterglow of catching his whopper bass had not yet faded when Frank got Jake's frantic call that Tuesday afternoon. "Drop everything, Frank, and get over here right now!"

What a change from yesterday when Jake surprised him by calmly listening while Frank explained the concepts of bottlenecks and the occasional need to do something radical—like allowing some workers and machines to sit idle (or at least to do something more useful). When Frank explained how this approach actually sped up production—of the right items at the right time—while simultaneously reducing the costs of in-process inventory, his boss seemed to consider his words carefully.

Jake hadn't even flinched when Frank confessed that they had taken some of the old, manually operated machines out of the company dump and were using them to off-load the new machines that had been the bottlenecks in production. In fact, Jake even pressed Frank for more details. It had been the longest and calmest meeting Frank had ever had with Jake. Well, that was then and this was now. Apparently things were back to normal.

"Exactly where are you, Jake?"

"The boardroom at the OAR Enterprises Building. Know where it is?"

"I'll find it," Frank said.

"Make it snappy," Jake hollered, hanging up.

Fishy Business

When Frank arrived at the OAR Enterprises Building, he was immediately escorted to the boardroom. Although he had never set foot in the building, he knew that it was from here that reclusive millionaire Oliver Reynolds reigned over a vast corporate empire. For now, though, his mind was focused on Jake. If he hadn't known better, he would have almost thought his call sounded like a cry for help. He had no idea how right he was.

The boardroom's oversized mahogany doors were opened by a young executive who identified himself as Ned. "Go right in," he said to Frank.

It was obvious that a high-level meeting was going on. And judging from what he could gather, Jake seemed to be right in the middle of it all. If Frank had ever seen a man on the hot seat, Jake was it.

"Frank! Frank!" Jake called out, taking him by the arm and leading him toward an empty seat. "Good to see you. I'd like you to meet Mr. Reynolds."

The dignified man sitting at the head of the table held out his hand and Frank shook it. "Hi, Frank," the white-haired gentleman said.

Frank hoped that the gasp he made wasn't audible. There, sitting in an Italian-tailored pinstripe suit instead of his usual plaid shirt, was the great man himself—Oliver A. Reynolds, known simply as O.A. to his fishing buddies.

O.A. and several others grilled Jake for several minutes. Whenever Jake found it difficult to answer questions concerning "his" new policy of allowing workers and machines to remain idle, Frank stepped in with the answer.

 Give credit where it's due.

■　■　■

Take credit for others' efforts at your own risk.

After the meeting ended, the participants funneled out through the two large double doors. "Oh, Frank," O.A. called out as he was leaving, "are we still on for bass fishing next Saturday?"

"Uh, sure, O.A.," Frank said.

Jake's mouth gaped and his color turned pasty as he stared first at O.A. and then at Frank. He didn't look well at all.

Epilogue

The vivid blue sky reflected on the still water of the cattail-ringed bay as two anglers, seated in a small rowboat, cast out topwater lures. The deep-toned croaking of a bullfrog backed by a chorus of songbirds added a pleasant sound track to the peaceful scene.

"Why didn't you tell me, O.A.?" Frank asked, reeling in his line.

"Tell you that I just happen to own your company?" O.A. said.

"That would have been nice."

"Frank, think back and you'll remember that you and I pretty much confined our conversations to fishing. And, if I recall, that's just how *you* wanted it.

"Later, *much* later," O.A. continued, "Hank mentioned that he had done some consulting work for you. By that time, I didn't exactly know how to slip it into the conversation."

"I see your point," Frank said. "What's going to happen now?"

"You mean to Jake?"

Frank nodded his head. "I know he looked pretty ruffled at the meeting, but he does try."

"I know he does, Frank, and I appreciate your loyalty. But you and I both know that those were your ideas he was spouting, not his.

"Not only did we know it, so did everyone else in the room. Frank, I'm afraid that Jake was moved up a little higher than he should have been. You can't blame *him* for that. But don't worry, he won't be let go. However, he might have a little adjustment to make now that he's working for *you*."

Frank winced. "You know, O.A., there's something else I've been wondering about. You never told me how *you* got started fishing."

"No mystery. I've fished since I was a kid," O.A. said. "As a matter of fact, old Hank was my best buddy and fishing pal.

"We were pretty competitive, even then. I was a real ruthless son of a gun, if you want the truth."

"I find that hard to believe," Frank said.

"Believe it," O.A. said. "Anyhow, Hank and I had a stupid argument and didn't talk to one another for years. It was my fault, but that's another story.

"The day after our big blowup, I came here to Lake Lindner to mull things over and try to understand what had gone wrong. Not just with Hank, but with work and a lot of other things. It didn't happen overnight, but I finally figured it out."

"Figured *what* out, O.A.?"

"I came to the lake to think; but I really learned *how* to think."

That was the best lesson Frank ever got from the Old Angler.

Afterword

It's clear that fishing helped O.A. learn how to think—not just on the water, but at home and at work. It became, in fact, *the* determining factor in his life. Let's hope Frank remembers this lesson.

Contrast this refreshing perspective to the approach taken by our business schools, and the messages contained within the never-ending stream of gimmicky business books that instruct us to choose from such tired old alternatives such as:

- Downsize the organization, and outsource some of the work.
- Wage a price "war" against the competition.
- Bring in a new "general" (CEO) and redirect the "troops."
- Ready the Golden Parachutes and find a buyer for the company.

These alternatives follow a predictable—and in most cases, counterproductive—pattern. Business should be more than form-

Afterword

ing arbitrary lists and computing cost benefits with little or no regard to the individuals involved.

Real progress comes from real thinking—the type of thinking *Fishy Business* espouses. Remember the story about the Japanese and their new and novel approach to designing a chemical plant? Had they restricted their choices to the ordinary and conventional, they would have built yet one more ordinary and conventional plant. Instead, they dared to "venture outside the box." This is only possible if we change the way we think through the establishment of a new and broader array of analogies.

Fishing or just reading about fishing experiences can help. Although the current business scene emphasizes the war-and-games approach, we are convinced that everyday life is a lot more like fishing—or should be. We hope you agree.

The Old Angler's Fishing Glossary

anchor   A heavy object—attached by rope, cable or chain—used to hold a boat in place.

angler   One who fishes with an angle (hook).

bait   (1) Live or edible fish food. (2) Fishing lure.

baitfish   Small fish eaten by predatory fish.

baitcasting reel   A revolving spool reel often used for heavy fishing.

bar   A ridge of submerged land.

bass   A large member of the sunfish family, such as the large-mouth bass.

bass boat   A low-profile watercraft outfitted with a powerful outboard motor; designed to be used primarily on large bodies of water.

bay   A shoreline indentation.

bed   A scooped-out portion of lake bottom into which fish lay eggs.

Glossary

bend (1) A curve in a fishing rod caused by the weight of a fish. (2) The place on a creek or river that turns.

bewhiskered An adjective that describes the appearance of a barbeled or "whiskered" fish. Whiskers or barbels, found on catfish and carp, are sometimes called feelers.

bluegill A flat-bodied member of the panfish family, larger than a pumpkinseed and smaller than a bass.

bobber A float used to suspend bait at a specific depth and indicate nibbles or bites.

bow (1) A bend in a fishing rod. (2) Bending at the waist to prevent line break-off when fighting a large fish such as a tarpon. (3) Front section of a boat.

breakline The point where water depth increases.

bucket A container (often five-gallon size) used by shore and ice fishermen to sit on and store supplies.

bugle-mouth bass A colloquial (and generally derogatory) term for carp.

bump (1) A tap, nibble, or nudge produced by a fish making contact with a bait or lure. (2) Small raised portion of lake bottom.

buzzbait A topwater lure equipped with revolving blades that is "buzzed" back across the water's surface.

carp A large member of the minnow family. Generally held in low regard in America, it is prized in Europe and Asia for sport and food.

cast One of several methods used to toss or throw bait or lures out.

catfish One of many types of barbeled fish, so named because of their catlike facial "whiskers."

cattail A tall, slender type of aquatic plant topped off by a brown cigar-shaped seed spike perched upon a long stem.

channel (1) A strip of water connecting two larger bodies of water. (2) A stream that has been covered by the creation of a reservoir.

Glossary

channel catfish A sleek, spirited fork-tailed member of the catfish family.

cold front Cold air that results in poor fishing.

(The) Compleat Angler A reference to Isaak Walton's 1653 book of the same name.

corn One of many "grocery store baits" used by carp anglers.

cover Natural or man-made objects used as protection by prey or ambush points by predatory fish.

crank The motion of turning a reel's handle to bring in a lure or fish.

crankbait A lure that derives movement and retrieval depth chiefly through its design.

crappie A speckled large-mouthed member of the sunfish family.

depth finder A sonar unit (sometimes called "fish finder") that displays the contours of the lake bottom and fish within that area.

"do-nothing" method A method of fishing that uses little or no lure movement to encourage strikes from skittish or inactive fish.

double haul Technique used by fly fishermen to increase the distance of casts.

downriggers Mechanical device used to take and keep a heavy weight at a specific depth. Bait or lures are fished behind the downrigger's weight.

drag A reel's mechanical device that permits a specific amount of slippage to prevent line break-off.

eggs Bluegills may deposit more than 30,000 eggs that are guarded by the male.

electric (trolling) motor Bow or stern-mounted battery-operated motor used in conjunction with casting or trolling.

feeding stations Specific spots on a stream where trout set up and wait for food to come to them on the current.

Glossary

flasher A circular-faced depth finder that indicates lake-bottom depth via bands of varying widths.

fly A lightweight hook, often made of feather or fur, designed to be cast with a fly rod.

fly rod A fishing rod designed to cast lightweight lures (flies) by means of a heavy fly line.

guide (1) A fisherman hired to help an angler catch fish. (2) Circular line holder of a fishing rod.

hawg Colloquial term for big bass.

hit The act of a fish striking or attempting to feed on a bait or lure.

holders A fishing-rod receptacle.

hole hopping The practice some ice fishermen use in moving quickly from one hole to another in search of fish.

hook A bent or curved section of metal with an eye on one end and a point on the other. Early hooks were based on a simple angled design that derived from a straight piece of wood, shell, or bone called a gorge.

hookset Pulling back on the rod to hook a fish.

hook size Numbers are used in reverse order to indicate the sizes of freshwater hooks. A size fourteen hook, for example, would be very small, while a size two would be much larger.

huggy baits Lures that have become temporarily attached due to storage in a common area.

ice fishing Winter fishing through a lake's frozen surface.

ice-fishing rod A generally short rod used by ice fishermen.

ice rod See above.

ice shanty A small shed used by ice fishermen.

ice spikes Pointed objects that may be jabbed into the ice in order to get oneself out of the water.

jig (1) A lead-headed lure with a tail of some sort attached as an attractor. (2) An up-and-down motion used to lure fish.

Glossary

jigging spoon A flattened metal lure that is vertically fished.

knots Any of a large number of methods used to secure fishing line to a hook or reel spool.

largemouth bass This large member of the sunfish family is one of America's favorite sport fish.

launch site The area where boats are taken in and out of the water.

lever-drag reel The drag system, mounted on the reel's side, may be adjusted by simply moving the lever ahead or back.

lily pads Flat-leafed floating vegetation.

limit The minimum length or maximum number of fish an angler may catch.

livewell A portable or built-in aerated container that is used to hold live fish.

lure An artificial fish enticer that may or may not resemble natural prey.

maggots Popular in England, fly larvae are not as widely used in the United States.

mako Fast, high-jumping, aggressive shark that prefers warm climates.

minnow (1) Any of 250 species of related fish, ranging in size from small (such as the emerald shiner) to large (such as the carp). (2) Any small fish.

monofilament line Nylon fishing line.

motor oil One of many soft-plastic lure colors; others include bubblegum, pumpkinseed, and tequila sunrise.

multispecies approach A tactic in which the angler opts to fish for any of several different species to increase chances of success.

nest A scooped-out portion of lake bottom in which fish eggs are laid.

nibble A faint or halfhearted hit or strike.

northern Shortened name for northern pike.

Glossary

northern pike A long-bodied, toothy fish related to the muskie and pickerel.

outboard motor A boat motor that is mounted outside of the boat.

outrigger Long pole extending from the boat's side which serves to widen the trolling path so as to frighten fewer fish.

overhead cast Vertical casting motion most often used by the majority of fishermen.

oversized minnow Carp, squawfish, and other large members of the minnow family.

panfish Pan-sized fish that include the bluegill, pumpkinseed, crappie, and red-ear sunfish.

panfish spoon Small, usually flattened, lead-weighted hook that is generally tipped with live bait. Known by many names such as teardrop, ice fly, or ice jig.

pattern Repeated modes of behavior that fish follow. Knowledgeable anglers observe and use these patterns to catch them.

pike See northern pike.

plastic worm An artificial worm used mainly for bass.

plug A wooden or plastic-bodied lure.

point (1) Hook tip. (2) A sharp portion of land jutting into the water.

polarized sunglasses Specialized sunglasses that help cut through the surface reflection of water.

popper A hollow-mouthed topwater lure.

portable livewell A movable aerated container that holds fish.

presentation The manner in which a lure or fly is offered to a fish.

rainbow trout Spotted trout prized for its fighting ability.

reel A device that attaches to a fishing rod and allows line to be cast, retrieved, and stored.

reservoir A man-made body of water.

retrieve The act of reeling in a lure.

Glossary

rig (1) The way a lure, bait, and other accessories are set up. (2) The act of setting up a lure, bait, and accessories. (3) One or more angling items used for a specific purpose.

rod A flexible tapered cylinder, usually constructed of fiberglass or graphite, outfitted with line guides and a reel seat.

roll cast A looping cast in which the fly line is not lifted off the water on the backcast.

rowboat A small boat with or without a motor that can easily be rowed with oars.

set The action of jerking back on a fishing rod to cause a hook to penetrate a fish's mouth.

shallow-diving crankbait A short-lipped lure that dives only a few feet deep when retrieved.

shoot line The ability to cast fly line a long distance.

skunked Catching no fish.

slack line Loose or limp fishing line.

snake Colloquial term for northern pike.

spincast reel A closed-face spinning reel often used by beginning or casual anglers.

spinnerbait A lure with a V-shaped wire body, equipped with a spinner blade at one end and a jig at the other.

spinning rod A rod used with a spinning reel.

spinning reel An open-faced reel used for relatively light lures and line.

spoon A metal or plastic spoon-shaped lure.

spud bar A long-handled chisel used to cut holes in the ice.

streamer A feathered fly-rod lure designed to imitate a baitfish.

strike A hit or bite by a fish.

submerged island An underwater hump or island.

tackle box A container in which lures and fishing gear is stored.

Glossary

tag A small marker affixed to a fish.

tarpon A leaping saltwater fish noted for its fighting abilities.

Texas style Rigging a soft plastic bait with the hook embedded in the lure body and sinker affixed directly above.

tippet A short section of monofilament line tied to the end of a fly line behind the fly or hook.

topwater bait (lure) A lure used to catch surface-feeding fish.

transducer Device that converts returning sound waves into electrical impulses which appear on the sonar screen of the depth finder.

trolling To fish by trailing a lure or bait behind a moving boat.

trolling motor A motor (usually electric-powered) that is used to troll or position the boat for casting.

trolling rods A stiff rod used for trolling rather than casting.

Troll Tiger Fictitious lure used in trolling.

trout Several species of fish prized by fly fishermen.

waxworm The larval stage of bee (or wax) moths; used to catch panfish.

water wolf Nickname for the predatory northern pike.

weedless popper Topwater lure with hooks designed to avoid snagging in vegetation.

weedy waters Waters with large amounts of aquatic vegetation.

whopper Large fish; also known as a "lunker."

wind knot A knot that develops in a fly line during improper casting.

woody cover Stumps, fallen trees or other types of wood objects used as refuge or ambush points by fish.

About the Authors

James P. Ignizio, a pioneer in the study of decision-making processes via analogies, served as Industrial and Management Systems Engineering Professor at Pennsylvania State University, and as Engineering Professor and Department Chair at the University of Houston and the University of Virginia. As a consultant to industry and government, he has most recently focused on the repair of reengineered and right-sized organizations.

Dr. Ignizio is author of six textbooks and several hundred papers. He is an associate editor of *Information and Decision Technologies,* and a member of the editorial advisory boards for *Omega* and *The International Journal of Computers and Operations Research.*

Dr. Ignizio was a Senior Flight Test Engineer, Research Scientist, and Program Manager for our country's aerospace industry. His contributions to the Apollo manned-moon landing program were recognized in 1980 with the First Hartford Prize awarded by the U.S. National Safety Council.

Bill Ignizio is an award-winning outdoor communicator who has written hundreds of articles for *Field & Stream, Fishing*

About the Authors

Facts, Sports Afield, Bassmaster, Cleveland Plain Dealer, and dozens of other publications. He served as contributing editor for *National Bassman, Florida Bass Fisherman, Outdoor Journal,* and *Fins and Feathers,* and has contributed material to a number of angling books.

A past president of the Outdoor Writers of Ohio, he often appears at outdoor shows, where he speaks on sportfishing. He has taught angling to adults and children, and he recently presented an angling workshop at the National Inventors Hall of Fame. Bill's sketches and cartoons have appeared in national magazines—and in this book.